The Fire Of God Series

**Elementary Edition
(3rd, 4th, & 5th grades)**

Year One

The Fire Of God Series

Elementary Edition
(3rd, 4th, & 5th grades)

Year One

By

Gloria Clawson

ISBN: 978-1-5872-1712-8 (sc)
ISBN: 978-1-6655-2180-2 (e)

Print information available on the last page.

This book is printed on acid-free paper.

1stBooks – rev. 03/27/2021

About The Book

The Fire of God Series is an inexpensive way to equip God's children with His Truth. Created specifically for Spirit-filled churches, it covers important subjects that other curricula miss... *The Gifts of the Holy Spirit, How to Pray, Why We Worship, The Protection of the Lord,* and many others.

The Elementary Edition, geared toward 3rd, 4th and 5th graders, contains 52 lessons, which include actual NKJ version scripture (Not just references, so the teacher doesn't have to search as the class waits.) and activity sheets that require only pencil, crayons and a teachable spirit. The activity sheets are reproducible, so there are no student books to buy. This non-consumable resource can be used year after year and is perfect for Sunday School, Children's Church and even home schooling.

Other age levels will be available soon.

Acknowledgements

With thanksgiving to God for…

My spiritual mom, Ressie, for teaching me, so that I could teach others.

My sons, Forrest, Ian, and Coleman, for reminding me every day how important it is to equip our children with the Word of God.

My dear friend, Wendy, for being my biggest cheerleader and for always being there, no matter how far away "there" is.

My "sister," Nicole, for going through the fires with me.

My spiritual brother, Coleman, for being a constant inspiration for his dedication to the Word of God, at all costs… and *his sweet wife, Susan*, who never fails in her enthusiasm for God.

My "adopted" parents, Tom and Ashley, for all they do and for all they have done.

And especially my husband, Ken, for supporting me, covering for me, and loving me…especially when I "disappeared" for hours to work on this book.

**I have no greater joy than to hear
that my children walk in truth.
*3 John 4***

Table of Contents

FRUIT OF THE SPIRIT

GIFTS OF THE HOLY SPIRIT

WITNESSING TO THE WORLD

PROTECTION OF THE LORD

Sample Class Structure

1) Opening prayer

2) Short explanation of the day's lesson

3) Story showing lesson, followed by relevant scriptures. The scriptures are there mainly for the teacher, however, they may also be used to ask or answer questions from the students.

4) Discussion questions - Each question is followed by a possible "answer" in parentheses. These "answers" are only meant to help the teacher guide the discussion. They are not meant to be exhaustive or the only "correct answers." Many questions are opinion type questions. Encourage the students to think of all the possibilities. God is not afraid of questions. The more questions asked, pondered, and answered (or unanswered) the more the students get to "flex their spiritual muscles." Unanswered questions may do more to pique curiosity than the answered ones. And that is more likely to send your students to their Bibles, searching for the answers. The discussion questions may be the most important part of the whole lesson, especially if you can really involve the students. You can look to the reference scriptures for more questions, if needed. Be creative.

5) Activity reinforcing lesson- each need only pen, pencil, or crayons to complete.

6) Scripture of the week - child takes home scripture and is encouraged to see how many times they can use it during the week

7) Departing prayer - using the scripture, where possible.

(Depending on how much time you have, a time of praise and worship, allowing the children to praise God freely, would be a great way to begin or end the class.)

Is God Real?

Lesson One

Lesson: The Bible is the basis for all of Christianity. Although Christ's life on earth only lasted for thirty-three years and His active ministry was about three years long, [1] His impact on the world continues. Our money says "In God, we trust." Our laws are based on His teachings. Even the way we figure out what year it is reflects His year of birth. But, what if there was no Bible? What if no one listened to the Holy Spirit and wrote down God's word? [2]

Look around. Look at a flower. Look at the starry sky. Look at your own hand. What else but a supernatural being, as wonderful as our God, could create such detail that works? Everything in your body, everything in the world, even the universe around you, works together like a well-oiled machine. Your heart knows how many times to beat a minute to keep the right amount of oxygen filled blood flowing to all parts of your body. Your lungs know how many breaths they need to take to keep the oxygen level in your blood right. And your brain knows how to send the proper signals to your fingers when you think, "I want to write the letter Q."

What about evolution? Scientists say we all came from a big explosion that resulted in molecules forming into life... that eventually became us. Life supposedly started as little wiggly things, then over billions of years formed into fish with legs, then eventually into monkeys which finally evolved into humans. Yeah, right.

It was a miraculous transformation from nothing to something. Miraculous is right. Nothing to something is right. But science is science, right? They can prove it, so it must be true.

OK. Prove it. The "theory" of evolution is just a theory. That means it has never been proven. But, what about what humans are made of? If you look at what our bodies are actually made of you get a bunch of things from the ground. So, we must have evolved from the earth, right? Wrong. We didn't "evolve" from dirt. We were created from it. Remember Adam? He was made from a handful of dirt. [3] And if man "evolved" from monkeys, why are there still monkeys? If evolution is supposed to be the survival of the fittest... if only the creatures who had the best features, those with the right stuff to survive, made it... why would there still be monkeys?

But, they try to teach evolution as if it is fact. Sure, they do. At one time they taught that the universe, including the sun, revolved around the earth. When a "scientist" tried to prove that the other scientists were wrong, they killed him. Medical scientists used to attach leaches to sick people to suck the "bad" blood out. It was a scientific "fact" that bloodletting cured illnesses. They killed a lot of people with that little "fact" of theirs.

Even Charles Darwin had a hard time buying into his own theory when he considered the human eye. He said, "To suppose that the eye with all its inimitable contrivances for adjusting the focus to different distances, for admitting different amounts of light, and for the correction of spherical and chromatic aberration, could have been formed by natural selection, seems, I freely confess, absurd in the highest degree."

And so, the devil is trying to kill more with this evolution theory. He wants you to believe that there is no God. If you don't believe, you can't be saved. If you aren't saved, you get to spend eternity in the lake of fire with him.[4] Misery loves company.

It is human nature to want proof for things. If you have proof, you don't really need faith, do you? Then again, the children of Israel, when lost in the wilderness with Moses, actually heard the voice of God thundering. In the time before stereos, you would think that God's voice, thundering from a mountain, along with all the special effects of lightning and the ground shaking, would be enough proof.[5] But, they chose to melt down all their gold and make a statue to worship instead.[6] Apparently, they needed something physical to hold on to. Even if it was something they made up themselves.

Maybe that is why some scientists are so bent on proving the theory of evolution. Maybe all they can believe in is something they have made up themselves.

Thank God we have God's works and His word to prove His existence to us. Put that together with your faith, and you have all the proof you will ever need.

Scriptural References

1. Now Jesus Himself began His ministry at about thirty years of age, being (as was supposed) the son of Joseph... Luke 3:23

2. All Scripture is given by inspiration of God, and is profitable for doctrine, for reproof, for correction, for instruction in righteousness,   2 Timothy 3:16

3 And the LORD God formed man of the dust of the ground, and breathed into his nostrils the breath of life; and man became a living being. Genesis 2:7

4 "He who believes and is baptized will be saved; but he who does not believe will be condemned. Mark 16:16

5 Now Mount Sinai was completely in smoke, because the LORD descended upon it in fire. Its smoke ascended like the smoke of a furnace, and the whole mountain quaked greatly. And when the blast of the trumpet sounded long and became louder and louder, Moses spoke, and God answered him by voice. Exodus 19:18, 19
Now all the people witnessed the thunderings, the lightning flashes, the sound of the trumpet, and the mountain smoking; and when the people saw it, they trembled and stood afar off. Exodus 20:18

6 Now when the people saw that Moses delayed coming down from the mountain, the people gathered together to Aaron, and said to him, "Come, make us gods that shall go before us; for as for this Moses, the man who brought us up out of the land of Egypt, we do not know what has become of him." Exodus 32:1

Discussion Questions

1) If God created us, why do people get sick? Did He mess up?
     (No. We did. Sin brought sickness into the world.)

2) What about the skulls of "early man" that they found. Doesn't that prove evolution?
(No. A handful of skulls prove nothing. They may be human, or they may belong to apes. Just because they found a few skulls that look different than the way most people look today does not mean that we came from apes. If they found a skeleton with a misshapen arm because of a birth defect, does that mean that at one time all men had misshapen arms? Remember the devil is a deceiver and will do whatever it takes to steal people's souls. If he can talk a few so called scientific experts into believing evolution, who in turn talk a bunch of people into believing evolution... look at how many souls the devil gets from one lie.)

3) What about carbon dating... the process that tells us how old things is?
(Again, this can't be proved. Scientist may take a vase, carbon date it, and say it is one thousand years old. But, since there is no one around that is a thousand years old, they can't prove that the vase existed a thousand years ago. Even scientists question the accuracy in carbon dating.)

4) What about dinosaurs?
(There are scriptures in the Bible that indicates that man and dinosaurs existed together.

"There were giants on the earth in those days..." Genesis 6:4
"Can you draw out Leviathan with a hook, Or snare his tongue with a line which you lower? Job 41:1

"Leviathan" is likely a sea creature. However the exact identity is unknown. The description of him sounds like a dragon or a dinosaur.)

Activity

Directions: Pretend that your best friend doesn't believe in God. Write a letter to your friend to convince him/her that God exists. Give personal stories of the impact the Lord has made on your life as "proof" that He exists.

God,

The Father, Son, And Holy Spirit
Lesson Two

Scripture of the Week:
But if I do, though you believe not me, believe the works: that you may know, and believe, that the Father is in me, and I in him."

John 10:38

Lesson: Are you confused? How can one Person be three People? The answer is... God is not merely a person.

We are made in His image. [1] And we are made up of three parts... mind, body, and spirit. [2] Your mind is the part of you that thinks... your intellect. Your body is obviously the thing that you cruise around earth in. Your spirit is the real you... the part that loves, the part that feels the joy of the Lord, the part that belongs to Jesus.

The three parts of God are sometimes called the Godhead. [3] They have always existed. As God was about to make man, He said, "Let Us (not "Let Me") make mankind." [4]

God is the One you probably always picture with the snowy white beard and the long robe. He is the Father... Papa God,... Daddy,... Father of the fatherless. It was His idea to create the heavens and the earth. He said, "Let their be light." And there was.

Then there is Jesus. Jesus is the Son of God. He was the one sent to earth to live as a man and die for mankind. [5] In exchange for all this, He was given all authority over the heavens and the earth. [6] God gave it to Him. And God gave Jesus all of mankind too. [7] When we pray to God, we do it in Jesus' name. If it were not for Jesus, we would be considered too "dirty" with sin to offer our lives to God. But, because of Jesus' sacrifice, we have become squeaky clean to God. As followers and believers of Jesus, we have become, in God's eyes, as sinless as Jesus. [8] Believing in Jesus and acknowledging His sacrifice is the only way to get to heaven. [9] Just believing in God won't get you there. Jesus is the Way, the Truth, and the Light. [10] Currently and forever He is reigning as the King of Kings.

The Holy Spirit... now this is the One that really confuses people. The Holy Spirit lived in Jesus when He was on earth. Jesus lived here as a regular person like you (except Jesus was the only Person who never sinned.) It was through the Holy Spirit, the Spirit of God, that Jesus was able to perform miracles. [11] The Holy Spirit is still here, performing miracles through followers of Christ. He is the Helper and the Comforter that Jesus promised the world. He will be with Jesus' followers forever, doing God's work through God's people. [12]

Still confused? Don't worry, this is one of those things that most people have trouble with. Just think of it this way: God, the Father, Son, and Holy Spirit, it's like having three Gods in One.

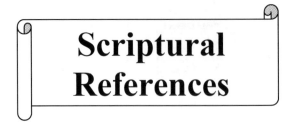

Scriptural References

1 So God created man in His *own* image; in the image of God He created him; male and female He created them. Genesis 1:27

2 Now may the God of peace Himself sanctify you completely; and may your whole spirit, soul, and body be preserved blameless at the coming of our Lord Jesus Christ. 1 Thessalonians 5:23

3 For in Him dwells all the fullness of the Godhead bodily; Colossians 2:9

4 Then God said, "Let Us make man in Our image, according to Our likeness... Genesis 1:26

5 He indeed was foreordained before the foundation of the world, but was manifest in these last times for you. 1 Peter 1:20

6 And Jesus came and spoke to them, saying, "All authority has been given to Me in heaven and on earth. Matthew 28:18

7 "as You have given Him authority over all flesh, that He should give eternal life to as many as You have given Him John 17:2

8 "Come now, and let us reason together," Says the LORD, "Though your sins are like scarlet, They shall be as white as snow; Though they are red like crimson, They shall be as wool. Isaiah 1:18

9 So they said, "Believe on the Lord Jesus Christ, and you will be saved, you and your household." Acts 16:31

10 For there is one God and one Mediator between God and men, the Man Christ Jesus, who gave Himself a ransom for all, to be testified in due time 1 Timothy 2:5,6

11 And the power of the Lord was present to heal them. Luke 5:17
"But that you may know that the Son of Man has power on earth to forgive sins" -He said to the man who was paralyzed, "I say to you, arise, take up your bed, and go to your house." Luke 5:24

12 "Nevertheless I tell you the truth. It is to your advantage that I go away; for if I do not go away, the Helper will not come to you; but if I depart, I will send Him to you. "However, when He, the Spirit of truth, has come, He will guide you into all truth; for He will not speak on His own authority, but whatever He hears He will speak; and He

will tell you things to come. "He will glorify Me, for He will take of what is Mine and declare it to you. John 16:7,13,14

Discussion Questions

1) Does God ever get jealous of the attention that Jesus receives? Or does the Holy Spirit get jealous of God? Do they get jealous of each other?
   (That would be like asking you if your feelings get jealous of your body. They share as one... and do not get jealous of each other.)

2) Can you just believe in God, but not Jesus, and go to heaven?
   (No. Jesus is the Way to heaven. Period. That is the way God made it to be.)

3) Why is Jesus the only Way to heaven?
   (Our own works do not get us to heaven. Only Jesus lived a perfect, sinless life. The wages of sin is death. He took away our sin. That means we have all "earned" death. But, because Jesus died for us, He took our place in death. But, if you do not believe in Jesus, that does not help you. If you believe in Jesus and are one of His, then God looks at you as if you lived a perfect life like Jesus. But, if you do not belong to Jesus, then you are standing there on your own, sins and all.)

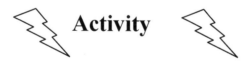 **Activity**

Directions: Look at the list below. Figure out Who did what (God the Father, Son, or Holy Spirit.) Then, list it under the proper Name. (Some things may go under all three!)

Has Existed Forever   Died for mankind's sins
Created heaven and earth   Lives in people's hearts, to guide them
Lived in Jesus   Loves mankind
Will return on the clouds   Is King of kings
Created man   Died for mankind's sins

You <u>must</u> have a relationship with to go to heaven
Gave the world commandments to live by
Lives in people and performs miracles through them
Enables people to speak in tongues

**An argument can easily be made that since God is One, all of these could be placed under all headings. Exploration on the part of the students should be encouraged. Therefore, no "right" or "wrong" answers are given.

Names of God

Lesson Three

Scripture of the Week:
And I appeared unto Abraham, unto Isaac, and unto Jacob, by the name of God Almighty, but by my name JEHOVAH was I not known to them.

Exodus 6:3

Lesson: Our Lord has many names. Each of these names reflects a trait. They describe part of His personality. But, He is still El-Elyon, the Most High God.[1]

Because we are sons and daughters of God, He sent us the Spirit of His Son to live in our hearts and call for "Abba Father." Abba Father is the part of God's personality that is the way daddies are supposed to be.[2]

Because we are God's children, we can come to Him as we really are. That means we don't have to pray in some fancy way… "Oh Lord…thou art the creator of mankind and I am your unworthy creation. But, grant me, Oh Lord… blah, blah, blah." You wouldn't talk to your parents that way. God reminds us that, because of Jesus, He can have a daddy-type relationship with us. So, you can just talk to him like a real person. "God, I really messed up. I lied to my parents because if I told them the truth, they wouldn't have let me do what I wanted to do. So, now what do I do?" God will listen. He already knows your heart. He already knows your real motivation – why you do what you do, usually before you even realize it. You can't hide your feelings from God, so you might as well fess up. Then, you can really listen to what He has to say to you.

The Creator made heaven and earth.[3] Who else but God could have pulled that off?

He is the Rock, His work is perfect; All His ways are justice, A God of truth, He is Righteous.[4] That means that nothing that happens is going to shake God. He's prepared for everything and He can handle anything. He is never – changing. His isn't going to love you one minute and then stop loving you the next.

The Lord of hosts is the Mighty One of Israel. He is a warrior who takes vengeance on His enemies.[5] Don't mess with God or God's people. He won't stand for it.

His name is Holy. He dwells in the high and holy place, He revives the spirit of the humble.[6] It doesn't get any holier than God. Remember that when you are in His presence.

The list goes on and on. Yahweh, the one true God, has many personality traits, just like you do. When He is called by one of these names, that part of God is being particularly glorified.

But, His name is not Buddha, or Allah, or Bahaullah. These <u>people</u> are not, nor will they ever be, God.

If your name is Timothy, your mom may call you Timothy or "the soccer player" or "the stubborn one." But, she is still talking about you. But, she wouldn't call you Rachel. Rachel is a completely different person. Unless, of course, you have a sister named Rachel. You know how moms are. She will eventually get to your name after she goes through the list of brothers, sisters, pets, coworkers, etc. But, she still knows who you are.

Do you know who God is?

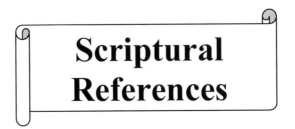

Scriptural References

1   Then they remembered that God was their rock, And the Most High God their Redeemer. Psalm 78:35

2   For you did not receive the spirit of bondage again to fear, but you received the Spirit of adoption by whom we cry out, "Abba, Father." The Spirit Himself bears witness with our spirit that we are children of God, Romans 8:15,16

3   I am the LORD, your Holy One, The Creator of Israel, your King." Isaiah 43:15

4   He is the Rock, His work is perfect; For all His ways are justice, A God of truth and without injustice; Righteous and upright is He. Deuteronomy 32:4

5   Therefore the Lord says, The LORD of hosts, the Mighty One of Israel, "Ah, I will rid Myself of My adversaries, And take vengeance on My enemies. Isaiah 1:24

6   For thus says the High and Lofty One Who inhabits eternity, whose name is Holy: "I dwell in the high and holy place, With him who has a contrite and humble spirit, To revive the spirit of the humble, And to revive the heart of the contrite ones. Isaiah 57:15

Discussion Questions

1) Why does God have so many names?
   (Each of His names reflects a part of Him. He has many sides to His personality.)

2) Don't all people worship the same God, even if they call Him Buddha or Allah?
   (No. Only the one true God, Yahweh, sent His Son to earth to sacrifice His life so that we may have eternal life. Without Jesus, there is no way to heaven.)

Activity

Directions: Pick out one of the names of God. Draw and color a picture that reflects that name. (It can be a picture of God or of something showing that part of His personality.) Below is a list of some of God's names.

Creator	Abba Father	Rock	Holy	I Am
Jehovah	Father of Lights	Living God	I Am	Eternal God
Almighty God	Everlasting God			

El-Shaddai (God of blessings)
El-Elyon (Most High God)
God of Hosts (heavenly army)

Why God Created Man

Lesson Four

Scripture of the Week:
God is faithful by whom you were called into fellowship of His Son Jesus Christ our Lord.

1 Corinthians 1:9

Lesson: Imagine the scene in heaven when the idea to make man first came up...

The throne room shone so brightly, the attending angels had to wear shades. There was a very important meeting being held. God, Jesus, and the Holy Spirit were there. The angels were in a buzz.

"What do you think it's about?" questioned an angel near the pearly gates.

"I don't know," answered another, as he flew up and over a nearby cloud.

"I heard they are talking about creating man," said a third.

"Man? What in heaven is man?"

"Oh, I don't think it will be in heaven," said the angel nearest the throne room door. "I heard Jesus saying something about creating a special place for this man."

"Well, why would They want to create man?" the angel wondered as he flew up to the angel near the throne room doors.

"I believe I heard Jesus say something about having someone to fellowship with. [1] "

"Someone to fellowship with? What about us?"

"Oh no. Man will be very special. God intends to crown him with honor and glory and put him in charge of His creation. [2]   Man will be created in the image of God, [3] " answered the angel, as he closed the throne room doors.

"Oohhh...," said the rest of the angels together. "In the image of God...," they each went their own way to think about this important event.

"So, You see, My Son," explained God, "that is the problem. If We create man, in Our image, and give him the ability to make his own decisions, he is going to mess up. And in order to make things all right again, You would have to go down there. [4] "

"I see the dilemma, Dad," answered Jesus. "But, You know, I would be willing to go down there and teach them. [5] "

"I don't know, Son, man will be stubborn. He will have free will, but he won't have the knowledge that We do. [6]   And they will never accept You."

"Some of them will, Dad. I can go down there and live as man, leaving my Deity behind. I am sure that if I live with them, as a man, and deal with the same things that they have to deal with, I can set an example for them. [7]   I can show them it is possible to live a Godly life as a man."

15

"But, God, what about sin?" the Holy Spirit asked.

"You know I won't sin," answered Jesus.

"No, I mean their sin," replied the Holy Spirit. "You know satan won't leave this creation alone."

"Oh. It is okay. I will take on their sin,[8]" said Jesus, somberly.

"Take on their sin!" thundered God. " The sin of the whole world will kill you![9]"

"I know, Dad. But, I know how much you want to have man to fellowship with. I can go down to hell, take the keys from 'ole Lucifer[10] and then join You guys again. It will be a great way to destroy everything the devil has done."

God thought about it for a minute. "Well, maybe. It sure would be nice to have man around, despite all the trouble. Son, if You will do that for Me, I will give you all of heaven and earth to rule and reign over.[11]"

Jesus smiled for a moment, then a look of concern came over His face, "Of course..."

"What is it, Son?"

"Of course, even if I go down there, once I am gone, there is no guarantee that man won't forget about me and follow satan instead."

"They will have My word, in print, the Bible, to guide them,[12]" said God.

"And Me," said the Holy Spirit.

"You?" asked God and Jesus together.

"Yes," replied the Holy Spirit. "I will go too. I can dwell within Jesus, the Son of man, acting as the Spirit of God. He will live on earth as a regular, mortal man. With Me living inside Him, He will be able to perform miracles.[13] Man will know Jesus is truly the Son of God. After He takes the keys of death away from Lucifer, I will resurrect Him. When Jesus comes back to rule and reign in heaven, He can send me back to earth to dwell in men's souls.[14] Whoever asks Me,[15] man, woman, or child, I will live in them, guide them,[16] teach them,[17] and continue Your great works through them.[18]"

God was silent for a moment. He looked at his Son, then at the Holy Spirit. Then He spoke. "You know, Son, even so, some will be lost, no matter what You do."

"My Father, I am willing to go to earth, suffer and die to save just one soul."

"And Holy Spirit, many will say You do not even exist and Your works are all dead. They will call the people you live within 'crazy zealots'.[19]"

"I know, Father, I know. But I am with Jesus. I know how much You want man."

After another long pause, God spoke. "All right, We will do it. We will make man. I will let You each go to earth to help him, when the time comes. But, when the time is right, Jesus, You will return to earth to gather our followers[20] and destroy our enemies.[21] This man We will create will bring us much joy, but he will bring us much sorrow. Heaven will celebrate for each soul saved.[22] But, We will grieve for each one lost. Let Us get some rest now. Tomorrow is a big day."

Scriptural References

1   that which we have seen and heard we declare to you, that you also may have fellowship with us; and truly our fellowship is with the Father and with His Son Jesus Christ. 1 John 1:3
God is faithful, by whom you were called into the fellowship of His Son, Jesus Christ our Lord. 1 Corinthians 1:9
"My sheep hear My voice, and I know them, and they follow Me." John 10:27

2   What is man that You are mindful of him, and the son of man that You visit him? For You have made him a little lower than the angels, and You have crowned him with glory and honor. You have made him to have dominion over the works of Your hands; You have put all things under his feet, Psalm 8:4-6

3   So God created him in His own image; in the image of God He created him; male and female He created them. Genesis 1:27

4   He indeed was foreordained before the foundation of the world, but was manifest in these last times for you who through Him believe in God, who raised Him from the dead and gave Him glory, so that your faith and hope are in God.
Peter 1:20,21

5   This man came to Jesus by night and said to Him, "Rabbi, we know that you are a teacher come from God; for no one can do these signs that You do unless God is with him." John 3:2

6   "For My thoughts are not your thoughts, Nor are your ways My ways, " says the Lord. "For as the heavens are higher than the earth, So are My ways higher than your ways, And My thoughts than your thoughts." Isaiah 55:8,9

7   For in that He Himself has suffered, being tempted, He is able to aid those who are tempted. Hebrews 2:18
For we do not have a High Priest who cannot sympathize with our weaknesses, but was in all points tempted as we are, yet without sin. Hebrews 4:15

8   But He was wounded for our transgressions, He was bruised for our iniquities; The chastisement for our peace was upon Him, And by His stripes we are healed. Isaiah 53:5
Because He poured out His soul unto death, And He was numbered with the transgressors, And He bore the sin of many, And made intercession for the transgressors. Isaiah 53:12

9 For the wages of sin is death, but the gift of God is eternal life in Christ Jesus our Lord. Romans 6:23

10 "I am He who lives, and was dead, and behold, I am alive forevermore. Amen. And I have the keys of Hades and of Death." Revelation 1:18
Inasmuch then as the children have partaken of flesh and blood, He Himself likewise shared in the same, that through death He might destroy him who had the power of death, that is, the devil, and release those who through fear of death were all their lifetime subject to bondage. Hebrews 2:14,15

11 And Jesus came and spoke to them, saying, "All authority has been given to Me in heaven and on earth." Matthew 28:18
"My Father, who has given them to Me, is greater than all' and no one is able to snatch them out of My Father's hand." John 10:29

12 All Scripture is given by inspiration of God, and is profitable for doctrine, for reproof, for correction, for instruction in righteousness, that the man of God may be complete, thoroughly equipped for every good work. 2 Timothy 16,17

13 Then Jesus returned in the power of the Spirit to Galilee, and news of Him went out through all the surrounding region. Luke 4:14
"The Spirit of the Lord God is upon Me, Because the Lord has anointed Me To preach good tidings to the poor; He has sent Me to heal the brokenhearted, To proclaim liberty to the captives, And the opening of the prison to those who are bound; Isaiah 61:1

14 "And I will pray the Father, and He will give you another Helper, that He may abide with you forever" John 14:16
"But when the Helper comes, whom I shall send to you from the Father, the Spirit of truth who proceeds from the Father, He will testify of Me." John 15:26

15 "If you then, being evil, know how to give good gifts to your children, how much more will your heavenly Father give the Holy Spirit to those who ask Him!" Luke 11:13

16 "However, when He, the Spirit of truth, has come, He will guide you into all truth; for He will not speak on His own authority, but whatever He hears He will speak; and He will tell you things to come." John 16:13

17 "But the Helper, the Holy Spirit, whom the Father will send in My name, He will teach you all things, and bring to your remembrance all things that I said to you." John 14:26

18 "But you shall receive power when the Holy Spirit has come upon you; and you shall be witnesses to Me in Jerusalem, and in all Judea and Samaria, and to the end of the earth." Acts 1:8

19 "the Spirit of truth, whom the world cannot receive, because it neither sees Him nor knows Him; but you know Him, for He dwells with you and will be in you."   John 14:17

20 "And He will send His angels with a great sound of a trumpet, and they will gather together His elect from the four winds, from one end of heaven to the other.   Matthew 24:31

21 "The Son of Man will send out His angels, and they will gather out of His kingdom all things that offend, and those who practice lawlessness, and will cast them into the furnace of fire. There will be wailing and gnashing of teeth. Matthew 13:41,42

22 "I say to you that likewise there will be more joy in heaven over one sinner who repents than over ninety-nine just persons who need no repentance. Luke 15:7

Discussion Questions

1) Why did God create man?
   (He wanted man to fellowship with.)

2) Why do you think God gave man freewill (the ability to make choices) when he knew man was going to mess up? (IE. Choose to eat forbidden fruit, choose to sin, etc.)
   (God wanted people to choose to love Him, not be forced to.)

3) What does Jesus mean when He says He is going to "leave His Deity behind?"
   (Deity is "the essential nature of God." He was going to earth to live as a man not as a God.)

4) Why do you think Jesus went to earth to live as a man when He knew He would suffer and die?
   (He knew it was what His Father, God, wanted and Jesus was obedient to His Father.)

5) What did God give us so that we know how to live a Godly life?
   (Jesus' life set an example, the Bible, which is God's word, and the Holy Spirit.)

6) Now where is the Holy Spirit?
   (He lives in the hearts of God's children.)

7) What do you have to do for the Holy Spirit to live inside you?
(Ask Him to and believe that He does.)

8) What do you think would have happened to <u>you</u> if Jesus did not come to earth and die for your sins?

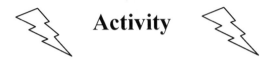

Activity

Directions: Each symbol represents a letter. "Decode" the message below.

God

is

faithful

by

whom

you

were

called

into

the

fellowship

of

His   Son,

Jesus

Christ

our

Lord.

1 Corinthians 1:9

Creation of the Earth

Lesson Five

Scripture of the Week:
The earth is the Lord's, and all its fullness,
The world and those who dwell therein.

Psalm 24:1

Lesson: In the beginning, [1] God created the heavens and the earth. He had made the decision to make man, now it was time to make man's home. Earth was a big mass of nothingness...dark, wet, and cold. The Holy Spirit hovered over the waters.

"Looks like we could use a little light, here, God," said the Holy Spirit.

God smiled. "I am getting to that, H.S." Then God said, "Let there be light," and there was light. Then He divided the darkness from the light. And He called the darkness Night.

"Much better, Big Guy. Now We can see what is going on here. What are You going to call it?"

"Let's call it a Day," smiled God. The evening and the morning were the first day. And they were finished...for the day.

With the Lord, one day is like a thousand years, and a thousand years is like one day. [2]

On the evening and the morning of the second day, God said, "Let there be a firmament in the midst of the waters, and let it divide the waters from the waters." And the universe was created.

On the third day, God gathered the waters together, with His word, and called them Seas. The dry land that appeared, God called Earth. God called grass and trees into being and commanded them to make seed and fruit, so they may reproduce and produce food. He took a long look at His creation, the earth, with all its oceans and land and grass and fruit trees. "I like it," He thought to Himself. And that was the end of the third day.

On the fourth day, God decided to make the seasons. So, He made the stars in the sky, so that people could look at them and tell signs and seasons, days and years. Then, while He was at it, He made the sun to light the Earth during the day...and the moon, to give a little light to the night. He liked what He did on that fourth day. The earth was almost ready for man... just a few more details.

The evening and the morning of the fifth day, God filled the waters and the sky with creatures. He made fish and dolphins, robins and sparrows. Then God blessed them, and told them to "Be fruitful and multiply." He smiled at His birds and His whales.

On the sixth day, God commanded the Earth to bring forth the animals... cattle and creeping things and all the beasts of the earth. Each was given the ability to have baby animals, like themselves. "Can't have doggies giving birth to kittens now, can We?" God joked to Himself.

The earth was ready for man. Then God said, "Let Us make man in Our image." So God gathered up a handful of dust from the Earth and molded it in His hands. Once He was happy with the way man looked, He breathed His breath of life into man's nose and Adam came to life. [3]

God had planted a garden eastward in Eden, so He put Adam there. He told Adam, "I have made every green herb and fruit tree for you to eat. You may eat from any tree in the garden, except the tree of the knowledge of good and evil. If you eat from it, then you will die. [4]" God warned Adam about it, but it was Adam's choice whether to obey or disobey God.

God told Adam that he (Adam) was in charge of all the living creatures of the Earth. Then He brought them all to Adam to name them. So Adam named all the animals, the fish, the birds, and the creeping things. [5] But, God saw that there was not an animal like Adam.

"It isn't good that Adam is alone. I will make someone for him," said God. [6] So, God put Adam into a deep sleep, took a rib out of his chest, then closed up his chest again. He took the rib and made woman out of it. Then, He brought the woman to Adam. Adam was very happy to have someone, like him, to share his life with. He called her Eve, which means "the mother of all things."

God was pleased with His creation. He made man and woman, to fellowship with. They had a beautiful Earth to live on with mountains and beaches, grass and trees, animals and birds. And they had each other. So, on the seventh day, God rested. He blessed the seventh day and called it Holy.

Adam and Eve lived very happily in the garden of Eden. They cared for the animals, which became like friends to them. Since the animals ate only plants then, (like they will again someday [7]) they all lived together in harmony. In the cool of the evening, they often took walks in the garden with God. [8] Life was paradise, just like God intended it to be.

Scriptural References

1 Genesis 1: Since a good portion of this lesson is derived from Genesis 1, each verse will not be listed. Rather, unless otherwise directed, you may refer to Genesis 1.

2 But, beloved, do not forget this one thing, that with the Lord one day is as a thousand years, and a thousand years as one day. 2 Peter 3:8

3 And the Lord God formed man of the dust of the ground, and breathed into his nostrils the breath of life; and man became a living being. Genesis 2:7

4 And the Lord God commanded the man, saying, "Of every tree of the garden, you may freely eat; but of the tree of the knowledge of good and evil you shall not eat, for in the day that you eat of it then you shall surely die." Genesis 2:16,17

5 Out of the ground the Lord formed every beast of the field and every bird of the air, and brought them to Adam to see what he would call them. And whatever Adam called each living creature that was its name. Genesis 2:19

6 And the Lord God said," It is not good that man should be alone; I will make him a helper comparable to him." Genesis 2:18

7 "The wolf and the lamb shall feed together, the lion shall eat straw like the ox, And dust shall be the serpent's food. They shall not hurt nor destroy in all My holy mountain," says the Lord. Isaiah 65:25

8 And they heard the sound of the Lord God walking in the garden in the cool of the day, and Adam and his wife hid themselves from the presence of the Lord God among the trees of the garden. Then the Lord God called to Adam and said to him, "Where are you?" Genesis 3:8,9

Discussion Questions

1) Why do you think God made the earth?
   (He created it as a home for man.)

2) The animals were friends with Adam and Eve. Why weren't the animals afraid of them or try to eat them?
   (The animals and Adam and Eve only ate plants. God made them to live in harmony.)
   Note: In the lesson of Noah there is further explanation of when people and animals became meat eaters and why animals now fear humans.)

3) Do you think one of God's days is the same as one of our days?
   (The Bible says one day is like a thousand years and a thousand years is like a day in 2 Peter 3:8)

4) What was the one thing God told Adam and Eve they could not do?
   (Eat of the tree of knowledge of good and evil)

5) Why do you think God told them not to eat from the tree of knowledge of good and evil?
   (God knew it would allow sin into the world.)

6) Do you think God knew that Adam and Eve would eat from the forbidden tree?
   (God knew before He even created the world that man would sin.)

7) Why do you think God put the tree of the knowledge of good and evil in the Garden of Eden?
   (This question goes back to man having free will. It isn't really free will if you aren't given choices. To eat or not to eat was the first important choice made by man.)

Activity

Directions: God created all the animals and Adam named them. Now it is your turn. In the space below create your own animal. When you are finished, name it and color it.

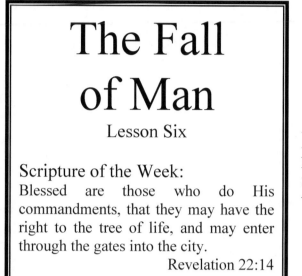

The Fall of Man

Lesson Six

Scripture of the Week:
Blessed are those who do His commandments, that they may have the right to the tree of life, and may enter through the gates into the city.

Revelation 22:14

Lesson: It was a cool misty morning. Eve had just awoken. She looked around for Adam. She found him sitting on a stone, overlooking a valley of green.

"Pretty day, isn't it?" he said to Eve.
"Sure is," she answered.
"I think I am going to head over to where the lions usually stay and see if that baby lion has arrived yet. Do you want to go with me?" asked Adam.
"No thanks. I was planning to go over to the river and take a little swim. But, if you want, I'll meet you in the middle of the garden. We can eat together."
"OK, Eve," replied Adam. "That sounds good. I'll see you soon."

Adam and Eve went their separate ways. Adam found that the new baby had arrived... a perfect little lioness. Eve took a nice swim. When she was finished, she started walking to the middle of the garden. She was almost there when she saw the forbidden tree. She had walked by it many times with Adam. And every time she wondered, "Why doesn't God want us to eat from that tree? He said if we did, we would die. But, why would we die?" Today she was alone. Or at least she thought she was alone. Then she heard a voice.

"Eve, did God tell you that you couldn't eat from the trees in the garden?" It was a snake talking to her.
"God said that we can eat from all the trees," she replied, "except this one." She pointed to the tree that the snake was in. "God said the fruit from this tree would kill us."
"Kill you? Nah... this fruit won't kill you. God just doesn't want you to be as smart as Him. He knows that if you eat this fruit, you will know all about right and wrong."

Eve thought about it for a moment. "Hmm," she thought to herself, " it does look pretty good. And I would like to be as smart as God is. "OK," she said, and took a bite, just as Adam was walking up.

"What are you doing, Eve?" asked Adam.
"I'm eating. Adam, I just ate from this tree and see, I am just fine. It didn't kill me. Here, it's pretty good. You try it."
Adam took a bite. "Umm, this is pretty good."

The snake smiled smugly. He was quite happy with himself. You see, he was really the devil in disguise and he had just helped sin enter the world.

25

Now Adam and Eve knew right and wrong. And with this new knowledge, they realized they weren't wearing any clothes. So quickly, they grabbed some fig leaves to cover themselves.

Later that evening, God came looking for Adam. He called out to him. "Where are you Adam?" God already knew that they had eaten from the forbidden tree.

Adam and Eve were hiding behind trees. Adam said, "I heard You coming, so I hid behind a tree, because I am naked."

"Who told you that you are naked? Did you eat fruit from the tree that I told you to leave alone?" God demanded.

Then, Adam blamed Eve, " Eve gave it to me. She said it was good and it didn't kill her. So I ate some fruit too."

Then God asked Eve, "What have you done?"

Eve blamed the snake. "The snake fooled me. He said it wouldn't hurt me, so I ate it."

God was angry. He cursed the snake, "Because you have done this, you will be more despised than any other creature. You will have to slither on the ground and eat dirt for the rest of your life."

Then, He told Eve that because she had disobeyed Him, having babies would be very painful for women from now on.

He turned to Adam and told him, "Because you have listened to your wife and ate from the forbidden tree, the ground is cursed for your sake. You will now work for your food, until the day you die."

God then made clothes for Adam and Eve out of animal skins then sent them out of the Garden of Eden.

Then He spoke, "Behold, the man has become like one of Us, to know good and evil. And now, lest he put out his hand and take also of the tree of life, and eat, and live forever..." God put an angel on the east of the garden and a flaming sword which turned every way, to guard the way to the tree of life.

Paradise was closed to Adam and Eve.

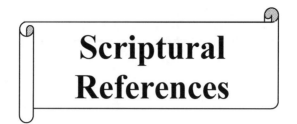

Scriptural References

The entirety of this lesson is from Genesis, chapter three.

Discussion Questions

1) Why did sin enter the world when Adam and Eve ate from the forbidden tree?
   (To sin means to commit an offense or to rebel against God. Adam and Eve committed the first offense against God by disobeying Him and eating something they were told not to eat.)

2) If the Garden of Eden was paradise, how did the devil get in?
   (The Garden of Eden was on earth. The devil had been kicked out of heaven, but he could freely roam the earth.)
   > **So the great dragon was cast out, that serpent of old, called the Devil and Satan, who deceives the whole world; he was cast to the earth, and his angels were cast out with him. Revelation 12:9**

3) When Adam and Eve ate the fruit, they didn't die like God said they would. Why not?
   (God did not tell them they would die immediately. However, death entered the picture with sin, because…
   > **"For the wages of sin is death…" Romans 6:23.**
   > **Because the sentence against an evil work is not executed speedily… Ecclesiastes 8:11**)

4) Why do you think Adam ate from the forbidden tree, even though God told him not to?
   (He ate because Eve told him to.)

5) Have you ever done anything that you knew you weren't supposed to do, just because someone told you to?
   (You may pose this as a rhetorical question, recommending that the next time someone tries to talk them into doing something they shouldn't, they should remember Adam.)

6) What was Adam's punishment for eating the forbidden fruit?

(Essentially, man was made to work for his food from that point on.)

For even when we were with you, we commanded you this:
If anyone will not work, neither shall he eat. 2 Thessalonians 3:10

7) Eve ate because she was tricked. Do you think you could be tricked into doing something that you <u>really</u> did not want to do?

8) Deception is a favorite trick of the devil. Can you think of ways that the devil tricks people today?

 (Lying, twisting God's word, blaming God for the evil in the world, "normalizing sin," for example "If people on TV do it, it must be ok..." What is "politically correct" is often not biblically correct.)

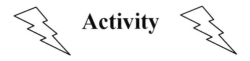

Activity

(**Teacher Note**: Explain to the students that the following activity will be for their eyes only. No one else will see it unless they choose to show it to them. So, they can be honest.)

Directions: Adam and Eve both blamed someone else for their own mistake. Think about a time that you have blamed someone else for something that you did wrong (even if they was also their fault.) Write about that time. How could you have handled it differently?

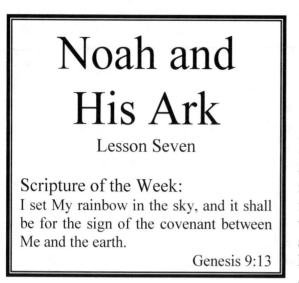

Noah and His Ark

Lesson Seven

Scripture of the Week:

I set My rainbow in the sky, and it shall be for the sign of the covenant between Me and the earth.

Genesis 9:13

Lesson: Many years had passed since Adam and Eve left the Garden of Eden. Now there were many people on the earth. But, the earth was filled with violence. God was sad. He was sorry that He had ever created the earth, and the animals and the people. He knew that people's hearts were full of evil, so He decided to destroy everything living.[1]

Except, there was one man on earth that wasn't evil... Noah. Noah was a good man who walked with God.[2]

So, one day God said to Noah, "I am going to destroy everything living on the earth. But, I will make My covenant with you. I will save you and your family. And I will save two of each living creature. You must build an ark." Then, God told Noah how to build this giant boat. He told him what materials to use and how big to build it. Then, God explained, "I will cause it to rain and there will be a great flood so that water covers the entire earth. Before the flood, two of each kind of animal will come to you. Keep them alive and bring them into the ark with you. Take food with you for your family and the animals."[3]

Noah was obedient to God and he built the ark.[4] Although Noah was 600 years old, he was able to do as God commanded, because God gave him the ability.[5]

Once the ark was finished, God told Noah, "Go into the ark now. It's time. Take your family and seven each of the clean animals and two each of the unclean animals, male and female. Also, take seven each of the birds of the air, male and female; in order to keep the species alive. In seven days, I will make it rain."[6]

So, Noah and his family and all the animals went into the ark. Then, God shut the door.[7] Seven days later, it began to rain, just as God had warned. It rained nonstop for forty days and forty nights.[8] The ark floated on the surface of the water for one hundred and fifty days.

Then, God made a great wind blow over the earth, causing the waters to subside. Exactly five months after the day the rain began, the ark rested on the mountain of Ararat.[9] The waters continued to decrease over the next three and a half months, until the tops of the mountains could be seen again.[10]

Noah opened the window of the ark and sent out a raven. It kept flying back and forth until the waters dried up. So, he sent out a dove. The dove returned to Noah, because it didn't find a dry place to land. Noah waited another week, then sent the dove out again. This time, the dove returned with an olive branch in its beak. Noah knew the waters had receded. He waited one more week and sent the dove out a third time. Only this time, the dove didn't return. Noah removed the covering from the ark and looked and the ground was dry. It had been one year and ten days since the rain began to fall. [11] Noah, his family, and all of the animals got out of the ark.

The first thing Noah did was build an altar to the Lord. Then he took of every clean animal and every clean bird (probably the offspring that had been born during the journey) and offered burnt offerings to God. [12]

God smelled the sweet smell of the offerings and said in His heart, "I won't ever curse the ground for man's sake again, even though the imagination of man's heart is evil. And I will never again destroy every living thing." [13]

God blessed Noah and his family and said to them, "Be fruitful and multiply, and fill the earth." It was then that God made animals afraid of man, because it was then that God told man, "Every living thing will be food for you. I have given you all things, like the green herbs." [14] Then he reminded Noah, "I will establish My covenant with you. I will never again destroy the earth with a flood. [15] As a sign of my promise to you and all of the people who live after you, whenever it rains, I will put a rainbow in the sky." [16]

And so it is.

Scriptural References

1   **Then the Lord saw that the wickedness of man was great in the earth, and that every intent of the thoughts of his heart was only evil continually. And the Lord was sorry that He had made man on the earth, and He was grieved in His heart. So the Lord said, "I will destroy man whom I have created from the face of the earth, both man and beast, creeping thing and birds of the air, for I am sorry that I have made them. Genesis 6:5,6,7**

2   **But Noah found grace in the eyes of the Lord. This is the genealogy of Noah. Noah was a just man, perfect in his generations. Noah walked with God. Genesis 6:8,9**

3   **And God said to Noah, "The end of all flesh has come before Me, for the earth is filled with violence through them; and behold, I will destroy them with the earth. Make yourself an ark of gopherwood; make rooms in the ark, and cover it inside and outside with pitch. And this is how you shall make it: The length of the ark shall be three**

hundred cubits, its width fifty cubits, and its height thirty cubits. You shall make a window for the ark, and you shall finish it to a cubit from above; and set the door of the ark in its side. You shall make it with lower, second, and third decks. And behold, I Myself am bringing floodwaters on the earth, to destroy from under heaven all flesh in which is the breath of life everything that is on the earth shall die. But I will establish My covenant with you; and you shall go into the ark- you , your sons, your wife, and your sons' wives with you. And of every living thing of all flesh, you shall bring two of every sort into the ark, to keep them alive with you' they shall be male and female. Of the birds after their kind, of animals after their kind, and of every creeping thing of the earth after its kind, two of every kind will come to you to keep them alive And you shall take for yourself of all food that is eaten, and you shall gather it to yourself' and it shall be food for you and for them. Genesis 6:13-21

4   Thus Noah did; according to all that God commanded him, so he did.
     Genesis 6:22

5   Noah was six hundred years old when the floodwaters were on the earth. Genesis 7:16

6   Then the Lord said to Noah, "Come into the ark, you and all your household, because I have seen that you are righteous before Me in this generation. You shall take with you seven each of every clean animal, a male and his female; two each of animals that are unclean, a male and his female; also seven each of birds of the air, male and female, to keep the species above on the face of all the earth. For after seven more days I will cause it to rain on the earth forty days and forty nights, and I will destroy from the face of the earth all living things that I have made.
     Genesis 7:1-4

7   So those that entered, male and female of all flesh, went in as God had commanded him; and the Lord shut him in. Genesis 7:16

8   And the rain was on the earth forty days and forty nights. Genesis 7:12

9   Then the ark rested in the seventh month, the seventeenth day of the month, on the mountains of Ararat. Genesis 8:4

10   And the waters decreased continually until the tenth month. In the tenth month, on the first day of the month, the tops of the mountains were seen.
     Genesis 8:5

11   So it came to pass, at the end of forty days, that Noah opened the window of the ark which he had made. Then he sent out a raven, which kept going to and fro until the waters had dried up from the earth. He also sent out from himself a dove, to see if the waters had receded from the face of the ground. But the dove found no resting place for the sole of her foot, and she returned into the ark to him, for the waters were on the face of the whole earth. So he put out his hand and took her, and drew her into the ark to himself. And he waited yet another seven days, and again he sent the dove out from the ark. Then the dove came to him in the evening, and behold, a freshly plucked olive leaf was in her mouth and Noah knew that the waters had receded from the earth. So

he waited yet another seven days and sent out the dove, which did not returned again to him anymore. And it came to pass in the six hundred and first year, in the first month, the first day of the month, that the waters were dried up from the earth; and Noah removed the covering of the ark and looked, and indeed the surface of the ground was dry. And in the second month, on the twenty-seventh day of the month, the earth was dried.
Genesis 8:6-14

12 Then Noah built an altar to the Lord, and took of every clean animal and of every clean bird, and offered burnt offerings on the altar. **Genesis 8:20**

13 And the Lord smelled a soothing aroma. Then the Lord said in His heart, " I will never again curse the ground for man's sake, although the imagination of man's heart is evil from his youth, nor will I again destroy every living thing as I have done. **Genesis 8:21**

14 So God blessed Noah and his sons, and said to them: "Be fruitful and multiply, and fill the earth. And the fear of you and the dread of you shall be on every beast of the earth, on every bird of the air, on all that move on the earth, and on all the fish of the sea. They are given into your hand. Every moving thing that lives shall be food for you. I have given you all things, even as the green herbs.
Genesis 9:1-3

15 Thus I establish My covenant with you: Never again shall all flesh be cut off by the waters of the flood; never again shall there be a flood to destroy the earth." **Genesis 9:11**

16 I set My rainbow in the cloud, and it shall be for the sign of the covenant between Me and the earth." **Genesis 9:13**

Discussion Questions

1) What do you think Noah's neighbors thought of him building this big boat? Do you think they made fun of him?

2) What would have happened to Noah and his family if he let peer pressure keep him from building the ark?
(They would have died along with everyone else and that would have been the end of mankind and the animals.)

3) Why do you think God didn't just build a boat for Noah and give it to him?
   (God wanted obedience from Noah. Noah in his faith and trust in God was obedient. Because of this, he and his family were saved. That reaffirmed Noah's trust in God.)

4) When the animals left the ark, God told Noah, **"The fear of you and the dread of you shall be on every animal."(Genesis 9:2)**. Why do you think that God made the animals afraid of mankind then?
   (Up until the time that Noah and his family left the ark, mankind was told only to eat plants. After they left the ark, God told Noah that animals would be food for him, too. He probably wanted to give animals a chance to escape, otherwise it would not be work at all for mankind to eat animals. Remember Adam's punishment for eating forbidden fruit was to work for his food. He had to till the ground and work for plants. This is probably an extension of this.)

Activity

Directions: Find the animal words hidden in the puzzle. When you find an animal word, mark through it (instead of circling it). Once you have found all of the words, try to figure out the message that remains. Use the space below to write the message. (Teacher note: The remaining message, which is also scripture of the week, is in bold italics for your use.)

E	*I*	W	H	A	L	E	*S*	*E*	*T*	E	V	O	D	*M*	*Y*
L	*R*	*A*	*I*	*N*	*B*	*O*	*W*	G	N	O	I	L	*I*	*N*	E
T	*T*	*H*	*E*	*C*	*L*	*O*	*U*	*D*	I	A	R	B	E	Z	S
R	*A*	*N*	*D*	E	R	E	G	I	T	P	X	A	P	E	R
U	M	R	O	W	A	K	O	A	L	A	O	B	*I*	*T*	O
T	*S*	*H*	*A*	*L*	*L*	G	K	W	A	H	F	M	*B*	*E*	H
F	*O*	*R*	*T*	*H*	*E*	T	L	G	O	A	T	A	G	O	D
J	A	G	U	A	R	A	⌘	E	W	O	C	L	T	A	C
S	I	G	N	O	F	B	*T*	*H*	*E*	Y	E	K	N	O	M
L	*C*	*O*	*V*	*E*	*N*	*A*	*N*	*T*	G	D	O	N	K	E	Y
A	*B*	*E*	*T*	*W*	*E*	*E*	*N*	*M*	*E*	O	M	O	U	S	E
E	G	O	O	S	E	N	E	V	A	R	R	L	L	U	B
S	*A*	*N*	*D*	*T*	*H*	*E*	*E*	*A*	*R*	*T*	*H*	F	M	A	R

Moses and the Big Ten

Lesson Eight

Lesson: The children of Israel finally came to the Wilderness of Sinai. It had been three months since their escape from Egypt and Pharaoh's army. They built camp at the foot of the Mountain of Sinai. [1]

Moses went up to God, who called to him from the mountain. God told Moses to remind the children of Israel what He did to the Egyptians.

God had sent lots of bad stuff to get Pharaoh to set the Israelites free. He sent lots and lots of frogs and locusts and hail. He even turned all the water into blood. But, Pharaoh still wouldn't let them go. So, then God got real serious. Moses told Pharaoh that God would kill all of the firstborn children of Egypt if Pharaoh didn't release the children of Israel. Still, Pharaoh refused, until it was his son who died. Finally, Pharaoh released his slaves. But, then, he had the nerve to send his troops out after them! So, God helped Moses part the Red Sea to allow the Israelites to escape Pharaoh's army. And once Moses and God's people were through, he closed the waters again a drowned the Egyptians.

God had a new message for His people. "I saved you and brought you to Me. Now, if you will obey My voice and keep My covenant, you will be a special treasure to Me above all people." [2]

So, Moses got together all the elders and told them what God had said. The elders of Israel agreed to obey God. So, Moses went back up the mountain to deliver the message. [3]

God then told Moses, "I will come to you in three days. I will come in a thick cloud, upon the mountain and speak to you so that the people can hear My voice and will believe. Tell them to get ready." [4]

The people got ready for God. On the third day the mountain was covered with a thick cloud, with thunder and lightning and the sound of a great trumpet. [5] The people were afraid, even though God had prepared them for what would be happening. Moses went up to the mountain to listen to God. It was then that God gave Moses the Ten Commandments, to give to the people. Here are those commandments.

1) I am God, the One who rescued you from the Egyptians. Put Me first in your life. Do not have any other gods before Me.

2) Do not make a carved image to bow down to and serve. In the days of Moses, people used to carve statues of animals and other things out of gold, silver, or stone. Then, they would worship these objects, as if they were God. Today, many things could be considered a "carved image"... money, friends, cars, computers. If you treasure anything or anyone more than God, it could be considered "serving a carved image." Even a little golden angel pin, if it is counted on for "luck" or "protection," could be considered a "carved image." As long as you put your faith and trust in God, instead of a "good luck charm," you will not be bowing down to or serving a "carved image."

3) Do not take the name of your Lord in vain. The Lord's name is holy. It is not a swear word.

4) Remember the Sabbath day, to keep it holy. The Lord rested on the seventh day. And He set this day aside as a day of rest for His creation. It is the perfect time to gather together with other believers and worship the Lord.

5) Honor your father and your mother. Honor is another word for respect. If you respect your parents, you will mind them, love them, and treasure them, like they treasure you.

6) Do not murder.

7) If you are married, remain faithful. If you are single, remain a virgin.

8) Do not steal.

9) Do not lie about or to other people.

10) Don't be jealous of what others have. Thank the Lord for what He has given you. [6]

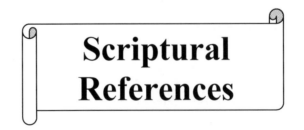

Scriptural References

1 **In the third month after the children of Israel had gone out of the land of Egypt, on the same day, they came to the Wilderness of Sinai. For they had departed from Rephidim, had come to the Wilderness of Sinai, and camped in the wilderness. So Israel camped there before the mountain. Exodus 19:1,2**

2 **And Moses went up to God, and the Lord called to him from the mountain, saying, "Thus you shall say to the house of Jacob, and tell the children of Israel: You have seen what I did to the Egyptians, and how I bore you on eagles' wings and brought you to Myself. Now therefore, if you will indeed obey My voice and keep My covenant, then**

you shall be a special treasure to Me above all people; for all the earth is Mine."
Exodus 19:3-5

3   Then all the people answered together and said, "All that the Lord has spoken we will do." So Moses brought back the words of the people to the Lord.
Exodus 19:8

4   And the Lord said to Moses, "Behold, I come to you in the thick cloud, that the people may hear when I speak with you, and believe you forever." So Moses told the words of the people to the Lord. Then the Lord said to Moses, "Go to the people and consecrate them today and tomorrow, and let them wash their clothes. And let them be ready for the third day. For on the third day the Lord will come down upon Mount Sinai in the sight of all the people. Exodus 19:9-11

5   Then it came to pass on the third day, in the morning, that there were thunderings and lightnings, and a thick cloud on the mountain; and the sound of the trumpet was very loud, so that all the people who were in the camp trembled. Exodus 19:16

6   And God spoke all these words, saying: "I am the Lord your God, who brought you out of the land of Egypt, out of the house of bondage. You shall have no other gods before Me. You shall not make for yourself a carved image-any likeness of anything that is in heaven above, or that is in the earth beneath, or that is in the water under the earth; you shall not bow down to them nor serve them. For I, the Lord your God, am a jealous God, visiting the inequity of the fathers upon the children to the third and fourth generations of those who hate Me, but showing mercy to thousands, to those who love Me and keep My commandments. You shall not take the name of the Lord your God in vain, for the Lord will not hold him guiltless who takes His name in vain. Remember the Sabbath day, to keep it holy. Six days the Lord made the heavens and the earth, the sea and all that is in them, and rested the seventh day. Therefore the Lord blessed the Sabbath day and hallowed it. Honor your Father and Mother, that your days may be long upon the land which the Lord your God is giving you. You shall not murder. You shall not commit adultery. You shall not steal. You shall not bear false witness against your neighbor. You shall not covet your neighbor's house; you shall not covet your neighbor's wife, nor his male servant, nor his female servant, nor his ox, nor his donkey, nor anything that is you neighbor's." Exodus 20:1-17

Discussion Questions

1) Why do you think God gave us commandments?
    (So we could live together, peacefully. So we would not sin against Him. So we would have an idea of what it takes to be happy (loving & worshipping God.)

37

2) How many things can you think of that people treat as more important than God?
   (Money, friends, clothes, toys, cars, jobs, school, etc.)

3) Although it is not bad to value friends and family, you should not put them above God. What are some examples of people putting friends and family above God?
   (Neglecting to worship God, because they are "too busy" with friends and family;
   Disobeying God's commandments because someone pressured you into it;
   Worrying more about what someone else thinks of you than what God thinks of you)

4) What are some ways that you can dishonor your parents?
   (If you misbehave in public, even if your parents are not with you, it will make your parents look as if they are not teaching you right. If you do not mind your parents, even if they don't know you are disobeying, you are still disrespecting them. Talking back, not being thankful for what they do for you, etc...)

Activity

Directions: "Decode" the pictures and fill in the blanks.

1) Have no other gods before Me.

2) Make no carved images to bow down to or serve.

3) Don't take the name of the Lord in vain.

4) Remember the Sabbath day to keep it holy.

5) Honor your Father and Mother.

6) Do not murder.

7) Do not commit adultry.

8) Do not steal.

9) Do not bear false witness against your neighbor.

10) Do not covet your neighbor's house, wife, or anything.

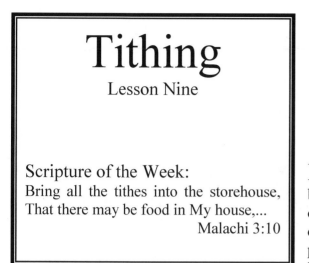

Tithing

Lesson Nine

Scripture of the Week:
Bring all the tithes into the storehouse,
That there may be food in My house,...
Malachi 3:10

Lesson: Your mom has just bought you a box of chocolates. You love chocolate. You open the package and are eyeing a cherry filled one when your mom asks, "May I have a piece please?" You start to say, "Sure!" But, then you look down at your box. You only have ten pieces and your mom wants one. That will only leave you with nine. What do you do?

You wouldn't have any of it if it weren't for your mom, you realize, feeling like you have been a little selfish. You hand her the box and hope she doesn't grab that cherry filled one. She grabs the one next to it. "Oh, thank you so much sweetie," she says, as if you had just given her a new car. You feel good. You made your mom happy and you got to eat the cherry filled one too.

You are sitting in church. They pass the collection plate in front of you. You just got ten dollars for baby sitting last night. Do you throw a dollar in? Are you going to share with God the way you did with your mom? After all, if it weren't for God you wouldn't even exist... never mind have the ability to earn money.

In biblical times, people gave the first ten- percent of what their fields and flocks produced to the Lord.[1] They also would dedicate people and things to God. As part of that dedication, they would give money to the church.[2] This is how God met the food and money needs of His church and ministers then. Tithing is still how God meets these needs today.[3]

Of course, you don't usually see a farmer pull his wagon up to your local church and unload six bushels of wheat on the steps. People usually just tithe money now.

But, what happens if you don't have money. Maybe you don't get an allowance and you are too young to work. What can you tithe to God? How about your time? God wants a tithe from the "firstfruits" of your labor.[4] There are probably a million things you can do to help the kingdom of God. Maybe you can volunteer to help in the church nursery or to help clean up the churchyard. But, it doesn't have to be at church to be giving to God. Maybe the special gift you have been given is singing. If you spend time singing at a nursing home, you have given God the fruit of your labor. Anything that you do to spread the gospel and love of the Lord Jesus Christ is considered giving to God. And until you have six bushels of wheat or maybe an allowance, tithe the "firstfruits" of your labor.

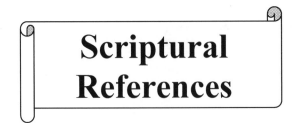

Scriptural References

1 'And all the tithe of the land, whether of the seed of the land *or* of the fruit of the tree, *is* the LORD's. It *is* holy to the LORD. Leviticus 27:30
'And concerning the tithe of the herd or the flock, of whatever passes under the rod, the tenth one shall be holy to the LORD. Leviticus 27:32

2 'And when a man dedicates his house *to be* holy to the LORD, then the priest shall set a value for it, whether it is good or bad; as the priest values it, so it shall stand. Leviticus 27:4

3 Bring all the tithes into the storehouse, That there may be food in My house, And try Me now in this," Says the LORD of hosts, "If I will not open for you the windows of heaven And pour out for you such blessing that there will not be room enough to receive it. Malachi 3:10

4 Honor the LORD with your possessions, And with the firstfruits of all your increase; Proverbs 3:9

Discussion Questions

1) What happens if you don't tithe?
   (It is considered robbing from God.)

   "Will a man rob God? Yet you have robbed Me! But you say, 'in what way have we robbed You?' In tithes and offerings. You are cursed with a curse, For you have robbed Me, Even this whole nation." Malachi 3:8,9

2) What happens if you do tithe?
   (You will be blessed. And God will chase away the devil for you.)

   "Bring all the tithes into the storehouse, That there may be food in My house, And try Me now in this," Says the Lord of hosts, "If I will not open for you the windows of heaven And pour out for you such blessing That there will not be room enough to receive it. And I will rebuke the devourer (the devil) for your sakes, So that he will not destroy the fruit of your ground, Nor

shall the vine fail to bear fruit for you in the field," Says the Lord of hosts;"
Malachi 3:10,11.

This is the only place in the Bible where God invites you to test Him about something.)

3) What if you really don't want to tithe?
(God loves a joyful giver. Giving out of obligation, rather than out of love is not what God has in mind.)

Activity

Directions: List as many things as you can think of to tithe to God.
What are some special things that you have to tithe to the kingdom of God?

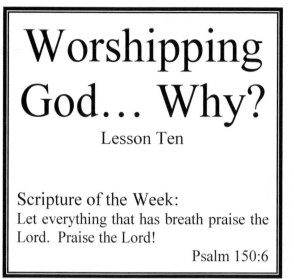

Worshipping God... Why?

Lesson Ten

Scripture of the Week:
Let everything that has breath praise the Lord. Praise the Lord!

Psalm 150:6

Lesson: Millions of people go to church every Sunday and sometimes Wednesday. Even more people confess the name of Christ and thank God, out loud, for everything from a good parking space to curing them of cancer. You hear all the time that you SHOULD praise God, but why?

First, there is the obvious. God breathed life into you. Without Him, you wouldn't exist. [1] And not only has He given you your life on earth, but through the death and resurrection of His Son, He has given you the opportunity for an eternal life. [2] And then there is all the rest of the really cool things He has done for us [3] ... our friends, our families, our identities, our talents. [4] The list goes on and on... trees, mountains, beaches, and animals. God gave mankind the knowledge necessary to invent cars, computers, and television. He led people to find cures and preventions for devastating illnesses. And when man's medicine fails, God often steps in and heals with the touch of His hand. [5] He gave Michael Jordan the talent to sink a ball, Walt Disney the imagination to create a fantasy world like non-other, and you the ability to affect the direction of the world. All of these things are reason enough to praise God. But, there is another reason... sort of a bonus side effect of praising God. You get to really tick off the devil. [6]

When God created Lucifer, He made him the most beautiful angel in heaven. His body was made like a musical instrument, covered with precious stones...diamonds, emeralds, sapphires. His anointing, that is, the reason God created Lucifer was to lead all of heaven in musical praise of God. He would have been able to stay in God's presence, by His throne, continually. [7] But, Lucifer decided that he was more important than God was. His pride destroyed him. God threw him out of heaven. [8] Then, as further punishment, God took Lucifer's job and gave it to the church.

Now, when people praise God, it paralyzes Lucifer, the devil. [9] When you lift your hands or voice to the Lord, it stops the devil in his tracks. The devil comes to kill, steal, and destroy. [10] When you praise God, you stop him dead. If the devil starts attacking you, using someone else's words (like someone talking bad about you), in the form of illness, [11] or any of the other bad things that he does, you can just start praising God. That devil won't stick around long when you start praising God. That's why satan usually tries to convince people that all the bad stuff in the world, God did. (Have you ever-heard people say "How could God have let such and such happen?") If people get mad at God, they won't be praising Him. Then, the devil can keep up the evil work. So, you can see, when you praise God, it isn't as much for Him as it is for you.

Praise comes in many forms...words, music, dance, and even schoolwork. Whatever you do, if you do it for God, that is a form of praise. Before Jesus came to earth people offered animal sacrifices to God. Now, however, our sacrifice becomes our praise. [12] Nowhere in the Bible does Jesus stop anyone from praising Him or God because they are "doing it wrong." [13] The good thing is, God knows your heart and He knows your intentions. [14] So, it doesn't matter what anyone else says about the way you choose to praise God.

The next few lessons talk about different forms of praise. In the meantime, whenever something bad starts happening, start praising God. Make that devil run for a change.

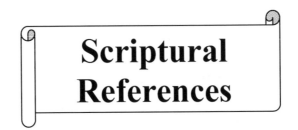

Scriptural References

1 **For You formed my inward parts; You covered me in my mother's womb. I will praise You, for I am fearfully *and* wonderfully made; Marvelous are Your works, And *that* my soul knows very well. Psalm 139:13,14**

2 **For God so loved the world that He gave His only begotten Son, that whoever believes in Him should not perish but have everlasting life. John 3:16**

3 **Every good gift and every perfect gift is from above, and comes down from the Father of lights, with whom there is no variation or shadow of turning. James 1:17**

4 **For the kingdom of heaven is like a man traveling to a far country, who called his own servants and delivered his goods to them. And to one he gave five talents, to another two, and to another one, to each according to his own ability; and immediately he went on a journey. Then he who had received the five talents went and traded with them, and made another five talents. And likewise he who had received two gained two more also. But he who had received one went and dug in the ground, and hid his lord's money. After a long time the lord of those servants came and settled accounts with them. So he who had received five talents came and brought five other talents, saying "Lord, you delivered to me five talents' look, I have gained five more talent besides them." His lord said to him, "Well done, good and faithful servant' you were faithful over a few things, I will make you ruler over many things. Enter into the joy of your lord. He also who had received two talents came and said, "Lord, you delivered to me two talents look, I have gained two more talents besides them. His lord said to him, "Well done good and faithful servant you have been faithful over a few things. I will make you ruler over many. Enter into the joy of your lord. Then he who had received the one talent came and said, "Lord, I knew you to be a hard man, reaping where you have not sown, and gathering where you have not scattered seed. And I was afraid, and went and hid your talent in the ground. Look, there you have what is yours. But his lord answered and said to him, "You wicked and lazy servant, you knew that I reap**

where I have not sown, and gather where I have not scattered seed. So you ought to have deposited my money with the bankers, and at my coming I would have received back my own with interest. Therefore take the talent from him, and give it to him who has ten talents.   For to everyone who has, more will be given, and he will have abundance' but from him who does not have, even what he has will be taken away. Matthew 25:14-29

5   For indeed he was sick almost unto death' but God had mercy on him, and not only on him but on me also, lest I should have sorrow upon sorrow. Philippians 2:27

6   Out of the mouths of babes and nursing infants You have ordained strength (praise), Because of Your enemies, That You may silence the enemy and the avenger. Psalm 8:2

7   You were in Eden, the garden of God; Every precious stone was your covering: The sardius, topaz, and diamond, Beryl, onyx, and jasper, Sapphire, turquoise , and emerald with gold. The workmanship of your timbrels and pipes was prepared for you on the day you were created. Ezekiel 28:13,14

8   "How you are fallen from heaven, O Lucifer, son of the morning! How you are cut down to the ground, you who weakened the nations! For you have said in your heart: 'I will ascend into heaven, I will exalt my throne above the stars of God; I will also sit on the mount of the congregation on the farthest sides of the north; I will ascend above the heights of the clouds, I will be like the Most High."   Yet you shall be brought down to Sheol, to the lowest depths of the pit. Isaiah 14:12-15

9   Let the saints be joyful in glory; Let them sing aloud on their beds. Let the high praises of God be in their mouth, And a two-edged sword in their hand, To execute vengeance on the nations, And punishments on the peoples: To bind their kings with chains, And their nobles with fetters of iron; To execute on them the written judgment - This honor have all His saints. Praise the Lord! Psalm 149:5-9

10 The thief does not come except to steal, and to kill, and to destroy. I have come that they may have life, and that they may have it more abundantly. John 10:10

11 So satan went out from the presence of the Lord, and struck Job with painful boils from the sole of his foot to the crown of his head.   Job 2:7

12 Therefore by Him let us continually offer the sacrifice of praise to God, that is, the fruit of our lips, giving thanks to His name.   Hebrews 13:15

13 I will not rebuke you for your sacrifices or your burnt offerings, Which are continually before Me.   Psalm 50:8

14 But the Lord said to Samuel, "Do not look at his appearance or at his physical stature, because I have refused him. For the Lord does not see as man sees; for man looks at the outward appearance, but the Lord looks at the heart," 1 Samuel 16:7

Discussion Questions

1) What kind of praise do you think God likes most?
   (Sincere praise.)

2) What kind of praise do you think the devil hates the most?
   (Sincere praise)

3) What are some ways the devil keeps you from praising God?
   (Distractions, lying to you to make you mad at God, etc.)

4) What are some distractions the devil uses to keep you from praising God?
   (Worry, self-consciousness, other people, tempting you to do things you shouldn't, etc.)

5) Can you think of lies the devil tells you about God to make you mad at Him?
   (He blames God for illnesses, deaths, failures, temptations, and even tells people God tested them to see if they would do evil, but God NEVER tempts people with evil.)

> **"Let no one say when he is tempted, "I am tempted by God"; for God cannot be tempted by evil, nor does He Himself tempt anyone. James 1:13.**

Activity

Directions: There are many things that God does for us. How many reasons can you think of to praise God? What are some things that you are thankful for? List as many things as you can think of.

Worshipping God With Our Mouth

Lesson Eleven

Scripture of the Week:

God has gone up with a shout, The LORD with the sound of a trumpet. Sing praises to God, sing praises! Sing praises to our King, sing praises!

Psalms 47: 5,6

Lesson: There are many ways to praise God with your mouth. One of the most popular is by singing. Maybe you have sung in church. Some songs are slow and some have a little quicker beat. But, a song doesn't have to be one that you have heard in church to be considered a song of praise. There are many Christian singers that praise God with their voices while singing country, rock, and even heavy metal Christian songs.

So, what is the difference between a "regular" song and a song that praises God? A song of praise is one that gives glory to God. That is, it shows to the world how great God is, while expressing gratitude for all that He does for us.[1] If you are singing about how wonderful Jesus is, then, as long as your mind is on Jesus, instead of what you are going to do after church, you are praising God.

You may have heard people praying in tongues. Have you ever heard anyone sing in tongues? It is a great thing to do when you don't know the words to the song everyone is singing or if you just feel like singing to the Lord.[2]

But, you don't necessarily need music to praise God. You can use words to praise God with your mouth too. You can say "Praise You, God, Alleluia," or whatever comes to mind.

And remember, church isn't the only place you can praise God. You can do it at church, at home, at school... wherever the mood strikes.

When you are talking to your friends, you can give God credit for the good that He does. For example, say you just made an "A" on the math test that you were really worried about and you are telling your friend all about it. "Thank God, I made an 'A'. I was worried about it. I studied and asked God to help me with it and He did." God does tests, you know. God will help you with just about anything. All you have to do is ask.[3]

You can shout your praises to God.[4] The devil REALLY hates that. "Shout in church!?" you ask. "Oh, I don't think that would go over too well with the folks." There is a time and a place for everything. Your church may have people shouting during praise and worship all the time. Or, then again, it may not. Remember that the Holy

Spirit does not do anything to disrupt. [5] So, if you feel the urge to start yelling "Praise GOD!" just as the pastor has everyone praying quietly with bowed heads ...it is probably not the Holy Spirit prompting you to shout. Then again, if everyone just finished singing a great, hopping praise song and they are clapping wildly, and shouting, and you feel like shouting too...go ahead. It may feel strange to you the first couple of times you do it. But remember, you would probably think nothing of shouting if your favorite sports team just won or if your mom said you were going to Disney World. God gave you life. What better reason to yell?

Praise is a powerful weapon against God's enemies. [6] Joshua and his army were told by God to march around the city of Jericho once a day for six days. Enemies of God lived in Jericho and God planned to give the city of Jericho to Joshua and his army. On the seventh day, God told Joshua to march his army around the city seven times, then blow a trumpet and shout to the Lord. They obeyed God, even though they may have felt a little silly doing it. And when they started shouting...the walls collapsed. [7] These were walls of stone that had stood for a long time. They were strong, but they were no match for God's people.

Paul and Silas, followers of Jesus that spread the gospel to Rome, were put into jail for preaching the word of God. They had been stripped, beaten, and put in shackles in the prison. But, still, they chose to praise God. From their cells they said prayers and sang songs to the Lord. All of the other prisoners listened to them. And as they sang out, the walls began to shake. It was like a great earthquake. All of the doors opened and the shackles fell off their feet. [8] Praising God set Paul and Silas free, like it can set you free. [9]

Your praises to God are not only a great way to thank Him for all that He has given you; they are a powerful weapon against everything evil in this world.

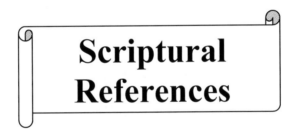

Scriptural References

1 Whoever offers praise glorifies Me; And to him who orders his conduct aright I will show the salvation of God. Psalm 50:23

2 What is the conclusion then? I will pray with the spirit, and I will also pray with the understanding. I will sing with the spirit, and I will also sing with the understanding. 1 Corinthians 14:15

3 Confess your trespasses to one another, and pray for one another, that you may be healed. The effective fervent prayer of a righteous man avails much. James 5:16

4 Be anxious for nothing, but in everything by prayer and supplication, with thanksgiving, let your requests be made known to God. Philippians 4:6

5   Oh, clap your hands, all you peoples! Shout to God with the voice of triumph! God has gone up with a shout, The Lord with the sound of a trumpet.   Psalm 47:1,5

6   For God is not the author of confusion but of peace, as in all the churches of the saints.
1 Corinthians 14:33

7   Let the high praises of God be in their mouth, and a two-edged sword in their hand, To execute vengeance on the nations, and punishments on the peoples; To bind their kings with chains, and their nobles with fetters of iron; To execute on them the written judgment- This honor have all His saints. Praise the Lord!
Psalm 149:6-9

8   You shall march around the city, all you men of war; you shall go all around the city once. This you shall do six days. And seven priests shall bear seven trumpets of rams' horns before the ark. But the seventh day you shall march around the city seven times, and the priests shall blow the trumpets. "It shall come to pass, when they make a long blast with the ram's horn, and when you hear the sound of the trumpet, that all the people shall shout with a great shout; then the wall of the city will fall down flat. And the people shall go up every man straight before him." Joshua 6:3-5

9   But at midnight Paul and Silas were praying and singing hymns to God, and the prisoners were listening to them. Suddenly there was a great earthquake, so that the foundations of the prison were shaken; and immediately all the doors were opened and everyone's chains were loosed. Acts 16:25,26

10 "Therefore if the Son makes you free, you shall be free indeed." John 8:36

Discussion Questions

1) Do you think God needs our praise?
   (No. God has angels praising Him continually in heaven.)

2) Why do you think God tells us to praise Him?
   (It is for us. We are made to fellowship with Him and praise Him. If we are not praising Him, something is missing. That is why so many people look for heroes to "worship." But, He also wants us to praise Him to punish the devil. Praising God paralyzes the devil.)

3) When Paul and Silas were in prison they started praising God. They were just about in the worst possible place they could be. Why do you think they were praising God instead of being mad at Him because they were behind bars?

(They praised God because they loved Him. Even though they were in prison, they could feel God's presence. They knew that no matter how bad things looked, God still loved them. They didn't stop loving God just because of the circumstances, just like God doesn't stop loving us because of the bad things we do. They also knew that Jesus suffered and they weren't going through anything that Jesus didn't go through Himself. Paul and Silas had no idea that their praise would cause God to collapse the walls of the prison.)

Activity

Directions: Complete the crossword puzzle. (Teacher note: The answers are underlined.)

DOWN

1) What do you do with your voice, set to music? <u>Sing</u>
2) The Lord is <u>Holy</u>.

3) Sound the <u>trumpet!</u> (a musical instrument)

ACROSS

1) God has gone up with a… <u>shout</u>
4) Whom did Jesus die for? <u>You</u>
5) You <u>must</u> believe in Jesus to be saved.
6) When you talk to God, you <u>pray.</u>
7) If you are baptized with the Spirit, you can pray in <u>tongues</u>.
8) When you praise God, you <u>destroy</u> the devil.

Worshipping God With Our Hands and Feet

Lesson Twelve

Scripture of the Week:
I desire therefore that the men pray everywhere, lifting up holy hands, without wrath and doubting.

1 Timothy 2:8

Lesson: Have you ever been in church and seen people lifting up their hands? These people are worshipping the Lord. It is a form of reverence and a way to feel closer and more in tune with God. [1]

The Bible gives us several examples of praising God by dancing to Him, too. [2] Some dances are to a lively beat and may be accompanied by tambourines or other "praise weapons." Some dances are slow, involving a Spirit-filled version of sign language. Still other dances are a combination of these. They may be carefully choreographed or they may be made up as the dancer goes along. In any case, a dance to the Lord is a very personal way to worship Him. Yet, at the same time, it accomplishes the same damage to the devil as any other form of sincere worship. [3] God inhabits the praise of His people. [4] So where there is praise, God is there. And the wicked perish in the presence of God. [5] So, evil cannot exist where God is. If you are praising God, the devil has to high tail it out of there.

King David danced to the Lord often. Once Michal (Saul's daughter... remember Saul who was in prison, yet praised God anyway and the prison walls fell) saw David leaping and whirling for God. She made fun of him and ridiculed him. David's response? "I will be even more undignified than this, and will be humble in my own sight." King David didn't care if he looked silly to her. His dance was for God. [6]

Like any other form of worship, dancing or lifting your hands to God may feel silly at first (especially if you have the devil whispering, "You look stupid!" in your ear.) Of course, the devil doesn't want to see you lifting your hands to God. He does NOT want you to discover the POWER OF PRAISE. If you do, that leaves him powerless against you. Because then, every time he tries to attack you, you will start worshipping God and paralyzing satan. God promises us that no weapon formed against us will prosper. [7] That doesn't mean that the devil won't try. That just means that he won't be successful in his plans for you.

So, what do you do when you start to worship and the devil won't leave you alone? The answer, as it always is, is to center your mind on Jesus. [8] Just keep concentrating on Jesus. If you have to picture Him on the cross, do that. If you want to picture Him on a throne, do that. Whatever it takes, just do it. If the devil keeps bothering you, trying to make you feel self-conscience, just do what Jesus did when the devil tried to tempt Him. Tell him, "Away with you satan, in the Name of Jesus!" Resist the devil and he will flee.[9]

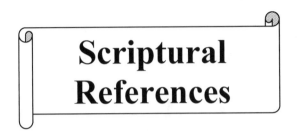

Scriptural References

1   I desire therefore that the men pray everywhere, lifting up holy hands, without wrath and doubting; 1 Timothy 2:8

2   Then David danced before the Lord with all his might; and David was wearing a linen ephod. 2 Samuel 6:14
    Then Miriam the prophetess, the sister of Aaron, took the timbrel in her hand; and all the women went out after her with timbrels and with dances. Exodus 15:20

3   Let the high praises of God be in their mouth. And a two-edged sword in their hand, to execute vengeance on the nations, and punishments on the people; to bind their kings with chains, and their nobles with fetters of iron; to execute on them the written judgment- This honor have all His saints. Praise the Lord! Psalm 149: 6-9

4   But You are holy, Enthroned in the praises of Israel. Psalm 22:3

5   When my enemies turn back, They shall fall and perish at Your presence.
    Psalm 9:3

6   Now as the ark of the Lord came into the City of David, Michal, Saul's daughter, looked through a window and saw King David leaping and whirling before the Lord; and she despised him in her heart. Then David returned to bless his household. And Michal the daughter of Saul came out to meet David, and said, "How glorious was the kind of Israel today, uncovering himself today in the eyes of the maids of his servants, as one of the base fellows shamelessly uncovers himself!" So David said to Michal, "It was before the Lord, who chose me instead of your father and all his house, to appoint me ruler over the people of the Lord, over Israel. Therefore I will play music before the Lord. And I will be even more undignified than this, and will be humble in my own sight. But as for the maidservants of whom you have spoken, by them I will be held in honor." 2 Samuel 6:16,20-22

7   "No weapon formed against you shall prosper, and every tongue which rises against you in judgment you shall condemn. This is the heritage of the servants of the Lord, and their righteousness is from Me," says the Lord. Isaiah 54:17

8   Draw near to God and He will draw near to you. Cleanse your hands, you sinners; and purify your hearts, you double-minded. James 4:8

9   **Then Jesus said to him, "Away with you, satan! For it is written, 'You shall worship the Lord your God, and Him only you shall serve.'" Then the devil left Him, and behold, angels came and ministered to Him. Matthew 4:10,11**

10 **Therefore submit to God. Resist the devil and he will flee from you. James 4:7**

Discussion Questions

1) People dance, clap, and lift their hands to the Lord. Can you think of any other ways to praise God with your hands and feet?

    (People can praise God with the work of their hands.)

2) When you start praising God, do you ever get thoughts in your head that distracts you? Why is that happening?

    (The devil is trying to keep you from praising God, so he can keep up his evil work against you.)

3) If praising God paralyzes the devil, why don't more people do it?

    (Many people don't know that praising God does anything to the devil. And others get too wrapped up in "religion" to relax and praise God in ways that God meant for us to praise Him. When Jesus lived as a Man, people praised God by dancing, playing all sorts of musical instruments, lifting hands, shouting, and clapping. That was the way God meant it to be. But, over the years, the devil convinced people that wasn't the way to act around God, especially in church. Of course he did. Those people were causing him way too much damage. Just look at how much more evil and demonic activity there is in the world today... and how much less worshipping.)

Activity

Directions: Make up a song (or cheer) and a dance (or cheer movements) to praise God. You can make it short and sweet, if you would like. Now, perform it for the class. Put some spirit into it! (Teacher Note: If you have shy guys, suggest that their song could be a rap song.)

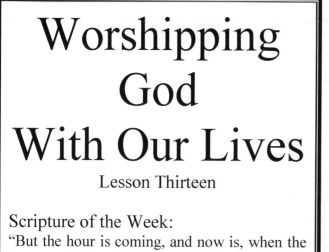

Worshipping God With Our Lives

Lesson Thirteen

Scripture of the Week:
"But the hour is coming, and now is, when the true worshipers will worship the Father in spirit and truth; for the Father is seeking such to worship Him.

John 4:23

Lesson: You can worship God just by doing what you do every day... going to school, hanging out with your friends, spending time with your family. Do everything that you do for the glory of God and you will be worshipping God with your life. [1]

So how do you do that? Let's start with the way you treat other people. Jesus lived on the earth as an example of how we should act. [2] Now, you will never be perfect, only Jesus lived a perfect life. But, God knows you will mess up now and then. You know the expression, it doesn't matter if you win or lose, it's how you play the game. Think of life in those terms. You will never be Jesus, but God gives points for effort. And in the end, as long as you have Jesus, you always win. Jesus told us above all else to love each other. He knew that if we loved one another we would be less likely to kill each other, steal from each other, and so on. Pretty smart guy.

It is easy to love people we like and to treat them well. But, what about when your little brother sneaks into your room and reads your diary...or when your little sister uses your homework as a coloring book? Your first reaction may be to pound them, or "pay them back." [3] This is when acting like Jesus gets a little tougher. What about when that geek who sits behind you? He just asked you to sit with him at lunch. Do you laugh at him and say "No way!" then make fun of him to all your friends? What would Jesus do? You can either bring glory to God or shame to yourself by the way you treat others.

The next thing you can do is obey God's commandments. Following His rules is a good way to honor Him. [4] After all, if you ignore or defy God, you can't be worshipping Him.

There is an old saying... "Your talent is God's gift to you. What you do with it is your gift to God." A very good way to worship God is to just use what He gave you, whether it be a wonderful singing voice, the ability to play football, your writing skills, whatever it is, you can bring glory to God with it. [5] You may have seen a puppeteer put on a show somewhere, and then afterward talk about God's gift of salvation. Or perhaps you have been to a Christian concert and heard a song that touched your heart. Did you see the Green Bay Packers win the Super Bowl several years ago? The first chance they got many of the players got on national TV and spoke of how Jesus changed their lives. Everyone has a God-given destiny. [6] Those who listen carefully to God and follow His path are the ones the world calls "lucky" because they are doing what they love to do. But, what they are really doing is worshipping God with their life. [7]

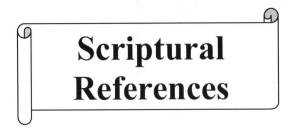

Scriptural References

1 Therefore, whether you eat or drink, or whatever you do, do all to the glory of God. 1 Corinthians 10:31

2 For to this you were called, because Christ also suffered for us, leaving us an example, that you should follow His steps. 1 Peter 2:21

3 Finally, all of you be of one mind, having compassion for one another; love as brothers, be tenderhearted, be courteous; not returning evil for evil or reviling for reviling, but on the contrary blessing, knowing that you were called to this, that you may inherit a blessing. 1 Peter 3:8,9

4 "If you keep My commandments, you will abide in My love, just as I have kept My Father's commandments and abide in His love. John 15:10

5 "By this My Father is glorified, that you bear much fruit; so you will be My disciples. John 15:8

6 For we are His workmanship, created in Christ Jesus for good works, which God prepared beforehand that we should walk in them. Ephesians 2:10

7 Therefore, whether you eat or drink, or whatever you do, do all to the glory of God. 1 Corinthians 10:31

Discussion Questions

1) If God knows that we will never be perfect, why should you bother trying?

(God expects us to do our best. He knows our hearts and He knows if we are trying.)

2) What should you do when someone has done something bad to you, like your little sister using your homework for a coloring book?
(Forgive them. It is okay to tell them not to do it anymore, getting your parents help too, if you think you need to. But, holding a grudge and doing something mean back will not help anything.)

3) Why do you think that God gives everyone talents?
(There are lots of things that need to be done for the kingdom of God, to bring in more people. God gave us each a part of the responsibility to bring people into God's kingdom. And He gave us each a talent or talents to carry out that job. He wanted us to enjoy ourselves as we do His work.

4) Can you think of ways to share Jesus with people who are not members of a church?
(You can treat people well ("Show your Jesus"), you can talk to people about Jesus, you can thank God around others, you can invite them to your church, etc...)

Activity

Directions: List all of your favorite things to do. Now, look at these activities individually. How can you use each of these to bring glory to God? Pick out two or three of your very favorite. Write down how you can use these to further the Kingdom of God.

The Power of the Name of Jesus

Lesson Fourteen

Scripture of the Week:

"And whatever you ask in My name, that I will do, that the Father may be glorified in the Son.
John 14:13

Lesson: Imagine having a weapon so powerful that it can move mountains, stop the rain, chase away evil, heal the sick, and change lives. Well, you don't have to imagine. You have such a "weapon," the name of Jesus.

Before Jesus left this earth He told his disciples, "Anything that you ask in My name, that you will be given." [1] He wasn't just talking to His first twelve disciples, He was talking to all of them. If you are a follower of Jesus, then you are His disciple.

The name of Jesus is above all names. [2] What does that mean? That means it has power. Jesus gave you the authority to do things in His name… move mountains, [3] stop the rain, [4] chase away evil, [5] heal the sick, [6] change lives. [7] The possibilities are endless.

So, how do you use the name of Jesus? It is very easy. Just say, "In the name of Jesus…" and then say whatever it is you are trying to accomplish. "In the name of Jesus, devil I command you to flee! In the name of Jesus, you are healed. In the name of Jesus, I ask you Lord to help me pass this test."

Of course, there are limitations. God won't do anything against His will, no matter how many times we try to get Him to. [8] Sometimes we pray for things that God does not want to do. Sometimes we find out why and sometimes we don't. Have you ever prayed for something and then found out later that if God had given you exactly what you asked for, it would have been a disaster. That is where you have to trust God to know what is best for you. [9]

He acts on your faith. [10] If you say, "In the name of Jesus…whatever," then you don't believe the "whatever" will happen, it won't. If you don't believe you will receive what you prayed for, you won't receive it. It is sort of a grown up version of not believing in Santa Claus.

And God won't do anything without a purpose. [11] If you walk outside and say, "In the name of Jesus, rain, sky, rain!" and it doesn't start pouring (which it probably won't), stop and think a minute. What would happen if it rained? Maybe the little boy down the street prayed that it wouldn't rain so he could go fishing with his daddy. Maybe if it rained it would be just enough water to kill off some farmer's crops. Now, why did you want it to rain? Just to test God, to see if the name of Jesus really had any power?

On the other hand, Elijah prayed that it would not rain for three years and six months and it didn't. He was showing to Ahab, an evil king, that God was the one true God. After the long drought, during which Elijah was fed by ravens first and a widow later, when God told him to, he prayed for rain again, and it rained. God had a purpose, to show Ahab that He is the one true God.[12]

The name of Jesus has real power… God's power to do God's will.

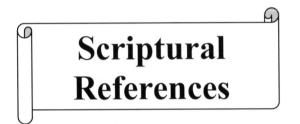

Scriptural References

1 **"If you ask anything in My name, I will do it.   John 14:13**

2 **that at the name of Jesus every knee should bow, of those in heaven, and of those on earth, and of those under the earth,   Philippians 2:10**

3 **So Jesus said to them, "Because of your unbelief; for assuredly, I say to you, if you have faith as a mustard seed, you will say to this mountain, 'Move from here to there,' and it will move; and nothing will be impossible for you.   Matthew 17:20**

4 **These have power to shut heaven, so that no rain falls in the days of their prophecy; and they have power over waters to turn them to blood, and to strike the earth with all plagues, as often as they desire. Revelation 11:6**

5 **"And these signs will follow those who believe: In My name they will cast out demons; Mark 16:17**

6 **"Now, Lord, look on their threats, and grant to Your servants that with all boldness they may speak Your word, "by stretching out Your hand to heal, and that signs and wonders may be done through the name of Your holy Servant Jesus."   Acts 4:29,30**

7 **They will perish, but You will endure; Yes, they will all grow old like a garment; Like a cloak You will change them, And they will be changed.   Psalm 102:26**

8 **For the LORD of hosts has purposed, And who will annul *it*? His hand *is* stretched out, And who will turn it back?" Isaiah 14:27**

9 Trust in the LORD, and do good; Dwell in the land, and feed on His faithfulness. Delight yourself also in the LORD, And He shall give you the desires of your heart. Psalm 37:3,4

10 So Jesus answered and said to them, "Have faith in God. "For assuredly, I say to you, whoever says to this mountain, 'Be removed and be cast into the sea,' and does not doubt in his heart, but believes that those things he says will be done, he will have whatever he says. Mark 11:22,23

11 This *is* the purpose that is purposed against the whole earth, And this *is* the hand that is stretched out over all the nations. Isaiah 14:26

11 Elijah was a man with a nature like ours, and he prayed earnestly that it would not rain; and it did not rain on the land for three years and six months. And he prayed again, and the heaven gave rain, and the earth produced its fruit. James 5:17,18

Discussion Questions

1) Does the power of the name of Jesus only work for His followers?
   (Yes, absolutely. If you do not believe, you do not have His authority. Without the authority of Jesus, you are not given the power.)

2) Why is it that sometimes even if you pray in the name of Jesus, your prayer is not answered?
   (Prayers are always answered. But, the answer may be "no." Or it may be "wait" or "if you..." God will not do anything against His will. And be glad about that. If he did, we might get some things that didn't work out nearly like we expected.)

3) What is the one thing that you <u>must</u> have in order for the power of the Name of Jesus to work for you?
   (Faith. Don't leave your prayers without it.)

Activity

Directions: Unscramble the words that describe some of the things that the power of the Name of Jesus can do. When you have unscrambled all of the words. Insert the words in parentheses in the puzzle below. You will find the Name that is above all names (Jesus).

1) (dugej))webneet tigrh dan grown : <u>Judge between right and wrong</u>
2) (leah) : <u>heal</u>
3) (ydserot) taans : <u>destroy satan</u>
4) vome (tinsomuna) : <u>move mountains</u>
5) ganech (slevi): <u>change lives</u>

Using God's Word

Lesson Fifteen

Scripture of the Week:
For let him ask in faith, with no doubting, for he who doubts is like a wave of the sea driven and tossed by the wind.

James 1:6

Lesson: If you buy a computer or a toy or even a car, the manufacturer includes directions. So, why didn't we come with an owner's manual? We did. Think about it a minute. Who is mankind's manufacturer? God is. [1] So that makes our owner's manual the Bible.

The Bible is full of examples of how to live, but even more exciting, it is full of promises God has made to us. Take a look at it. God has given us promise after promise. You just have to know they are there and learn to "stand on" God's promises.

Let's say for a minute that your mom promised to take you out for ice cream this Saturday. Saturday comes and everyone is busy doing "Saturday - things." Then, you remember your mom's promise. "All right!" you think to yourself. "Ice cream time!" So, you go find your mom, who is busy cleaning the bathroom. "Mom," you say "remember you promised to take us for ice cream." Your mom looks up at you, sponge in one hand, ammonia in the other. "That's right, I did. Well, you need to finish cleaning your room first. And I need to finish up here, then we will go." About an hour later you are on your way to vanilla swirl. Your mom made a promise to you. You reminded her of it and she came through for you. Now, she didn't drop everything and hand you an ice cream cone. Things had to be done before she could fulfill that promise. But, she did like she said she would.

God is like that. He has given us a book full of promises. He expects us to stand on them. In fact, He loves it when we do. That means you know the truth. [2] You can go to God with His promises and He will fulfill them. He may not drop everything and hand you what you ask for. You may have some things in your life that need to be taken care of first. He may need to do some other things too. But, He will honor His promise to you. The neat thing about God is, no matter what, you can count on Him. Your mom may realize that she doesn't have enough money to take your for ice cream after all. But, God isn't going to go back on His word. [3]

So, how do you stand on God's promises? There are no special formulas or magic words. Just pick up your owner's manual, the Bible. Find the promise that you need, whether it is for overcoming the bad things that come your way, receiving an answer to your prayer, [4] heavenly protection, [5] whatever it is, then read it out loud. Talk to God about it. Tell Him, "God, you promised this and I believe it. In the name of Jesus, I thank you for this promise. Or, in the name of Jesus, I claim this promise. Or, God, you promised me divine protection (or whatever promise you are standing on) and in the name of Jesus, I stand on that promise." There is no special wording necessary. Just remember to pray using the name of Jesus.[6]

So, you found the promise, then you prayed about it, now what? How many times do you have to ask God? What do you do next?

Don't worry, God heard you the first time. You don't have to keep asking to convince Him He keeps His promises. In fact, your prayers stay in the throne room of heaven with God.[7] The devil may try to convince you that God wasn't listening or that He isn't really going to keep His word. He may even try to make things appear worse after you pray.[8] Don't worry about appearances. It is the devil's job to try to make you doubt God. Just tell him to "shut up in the name of Jesus," and go on. If you need to keep asking God until **you** are convinced, that is fine. Or if it has been a while and you are beginning to wonder and you need to talk to God about it some more, go ahead. But, God always hears you the first time.

The next thing you do is just have faith. Believe that God will do as He says He will. Remember not to speak against what you just asked for either. Think about it this way... you have just asked mom if she would take you for ice cream Saturday. She says yes. Then, you put your hands on your hips, twist your face all up and say, "Sure you are going to take me for ice cream on Saturday! I don't believe you for a minute." And then what does your mom do? If she is like most moms, she will send you straight to your room and you can forget about having ice cream... maybe for the rest of the month. The Bible calls this being double minded.[9] You can't pray for something one minute, then talk about how lousy it is that you aren't going to get it the next. Faith moves mountains.[10] Doubt does nothing.

Remember that prayer is a conversation. It is a time to share with God, both the good and the bad things that are happening in your life. If you are talking to your best friend, you are not the only one talking. Your friend is going to talk too. Prayer is like that. God will answer you. You just have to learn His voice. He probably will not speak out loud to you, but He will speak to you. God speaks to us through the Bible, through other people, through dreams, and through our own thoughts. If you are ever in doubt about whether or not something is from God, check your Bible. God will never tell you something that goes against what the Bible says. The more you talk to God, the easier it is to recognize His "voice." God is never too busy, too tired, or too upset to listen to what you have to say. He is always listening.

Scriptural References

1   **Then God said, "Let Us make man in Our image, according to Our likeness; let them have dominion over the fish of the sea, over the birds of the air, and over the cattle, over all the earth and over every creeping thing that creeps on the earth." Genesis 1:26**

2 I have no greater joy than to hear that my children walk in truth.   3 John 4

3 in hope of eternal life which God, who cannot lie, promised before time began, Titus 1:2

4 For the eyes of the LORD are on the righteous, And His ears are open to their prayers; But the face of the LORD is against those who do evil."   1 Peter 3:12

5 Finally, my brethren, be strong in the Lord and in the power of His might. Put on the whole armor of God, that you may be able to stand against the wiles of the devil. For we do not wrestle against flesh and blood, but against principalities, against powers, against the rulers of the darkness of this age, against spiritual hosts of wickedness in the heavenly places.   Ephesians 6:10-12

6 "You did not choose Me, but I chose you and appointed you that you should go and bear fruit, and that your fruit should remain, that whatever you ask the Father in My name He may give you.   John 15:16

7 Now when He had taken the scroll, the four living creatures and the twenty-four elders fell down before the Lamb, each having a harp, and golden bowls full of incense, which are the prayers of the saints.   Revelation 5:8

8 For we walk by faith, not by sight.   2 Corinthians 5:7

9 But let him ask in faith, with no doubting, for he who doubts is like a wave of the sea driven and tossed by the wind. For let not that man suppose that he will receive anything from the Lord; he is a double-minded man, unstable in all his ways. James 1:6-8

10 So Jesus said to them, "Because of your unbelief; for assuredly, I say to you, if you have faith as a mustard seed, you will say to this mountain, 'Move from here to there,' and it will move; and nothing will be impossible for you.   Matthew 17:20

Discussion Questions

1) The Bible is a big book. How do you find the particular promise you are looking for?

(In the back of most Bibles, there is an index, called "concordance." You can look things up alphabetically in it. You can ask your parents or pastor. And if you have a computer, you can even look it up online on the Internet. If you really want to find it, you can. Just ask the Holy Spirit to help you. He always knows what you are looking for.)

2) What does it mean to "stand on" God's promises?
   (It means to believe God, have faith in His word, and to count on Him.)

3) Jesus told us **"When you pray do not use vain repetitions as the heathens do. For they think they will be heard for their many words." Matthew 6:7**
   Does that mean that we shouldn't ask God for something more than once?
   ("Heathens" do not believe in God. They pray to things that are not God. Your prayers are not in vain; they are full of spirit and life, because they are the promises of God. If you have to pray the same prayer a few times to help your own heart, God understands…even though He heard you the first time.)

4) Does God ever get tired of hearing from us? How many times can you ask Him for things?
   (God loves to hear from you. You were created to talk to Him. That is the reason He made man. We have limitless prayer through the Son, Jesus. Just remember to thank God for all that He does for you too.)

Activity

Directions: The Bible is full of God's promises. Name as many of God's promises as you can. Draw (and color) a picture of God fulfilling on of His promises

Teacher use : Here are some promises of God to get the students started, if necessary...

Abundant life (John 10:10), answer to prayers (1 Peter 3:12), blessings to liberal (Malachi 3:10, Luke 6:38), comfort (Isaiah 40 1:2), eternal life (Mark 10:30, John 17:2, 3, 21), Gift of the Holy Spirit (Acts 2:38), protection (Ephesians 6:10-18), peace (Philippians 4:6,7), remission of sins (Acts 2:38), strength (Ephesians 3:16), trials overcome (1 Peter 1:6-8), mercy (Titus 3:4-6)

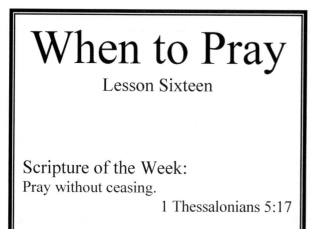

When to Pray

Lesson Sixteen

Scripture of the Week:
Pray without ceasing.

1 Thessalonians 5:17

Lesson: You learned in the last lesson how to pray and receive God's promises. What are some other reasons to pray?

God's promises are not just for our personal use. They are also for other people. One of the best things you can do for someone is to pray for them. Even if they do not believe, God can use your faith to fulfill a promise. In the meantime, that shows the unbeliever that God is real and He answers prayers. Jesus tells us to pray for one another.[1] It is pretty easy to pray for someone you like. But, Jesus also tells us to pray for our enemies.[2] That is when things get tougher.

What do you do if the kid who sits behind you in class... you know, the one who never takes a bath... what do you do if he has just stolen your really cool swirly glitter pencil? He denies it, but you know he did it. And you know you won't get it back. You pray for him. Uh oh! I have to pray for him? Yikes, that is tough. Try really hard to separate the sinner from the sin. He is one of God's children. Jesus loves him and died for him, just like He did for you. Yes, he stole from you and yes, he smells. Nobody is perfect. Jesus was the only perfect person.[3]

When are some other times to pray? You can pray when you are scared or feeling threatened. One of God's promises is divine protection.[4] That means protection that comes from God. He has a bunch of angels whose job it is to protect God's own.

You can pray when you need to make a decision and don't know which direction to choose. Since God knows your future, who better to ask about your next step? And since He also knows your past, who better to understand where you are coming from? The Holy Spirit is there to guide us and light up the next step.[5]

You can pray to thank God for something He has given you, be it help on a test or your heart's desire (whatever that may be.) God loves a thankful heart.[6]

Anything you face in life, good or bad, is a reason to pray. Remember that Jesus is always there and He is always listening. He wants to have a relationship with you. He wants you to talk to Him. Pray without ceasing, pray continually, just pray.[7]

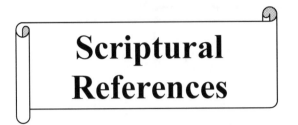

Scriptural References

1 Confess your trespasses to one another, and pray for one another, that you may be healed. The effective, fervent prayer of a righteous man avails much. James 5:16

2 "But I say to you, love your enemies, bless those who curse you, do good to those who hate you, and pray for those who spitefully use you and persecute you," Matthew 5:44

3 For we do not have a High Priest who cannot sympathize with our weaknesses, but was in all points tempted as we are, yet without sin. Hebrews 4:15

4 For He shall give His angels charge over you, To keep you in all your ways. Psalm 91:11

5 This also comes from the LORD of hosts, Who is wonderful in counsel and excellent in guidance. Isaiah 28:29

6 And let the peace of God rule in your hearts, to which also you were called in one body; and be thankful. Colossians 3:15

7 pray without ceasing,   Thessalonians 5:17

Discussion Questions

1) Do you always get what you pray for?

   (Not always. Although God answers all prayers, God's answer to your prayer may not always be "yes." You have to have faith that God knows what is best. He knows what is in your future.)

2) What happens if we don't thank God for what He has given us?

(How would you feel if you did something great for someone and they didn't even bother to say thank you?)

 **Activity**

Directions: Write a letter to God. You can thank Him, let Him know what you are feeling and thinking, whatever you want to talk to Him about. This is just between you and Him.

Why Jesus Came

Lesson Seventeen

Scripture of the Week:
For this cause I was born, and for this cause I have come into the world, that I should bear witness to the truth. Everyone who is of the truth hears My voice."

John 18:37

Lesson: Jesus came to die.[1] God gives each person a destiny.[2] Fulfilling God's destiny for us is our goal on this earth. Jesus is the only Person known to man whose life's goal was to die. Along the way Jesus was to be a witness and teacher of the Truth that is God. He was sent to live a perfect, sinless life and then die for the world's sins... some were sins that weren't even going to be committed for hundreds or thousands of years.

That means that two thousand years ago a little Baby Boy was born just because we were going to mess up and sin. His short life was spent learning and teaching about God. He knew when He was a young Child that Joseph was his stepfather. He knew that God Almighty was His real Father.[3] Imagine the attitude Jesus could have had knowing that God was His father. It kind of gives whole new meaning to the expression "My Dad can beat up your dad." Doesn't it? Yet, Jesus was obedient to His earthly parents. His life's work was obedience.[4]

Jesus knew His purpose was to die for us. He was given the choice of whether or not to obey, just like all people. In fact at one point He asked God if the whole cross thing was really going to be necessary. He asked God, "If there is any other way...." But, when it came down to it, He was more concerned with what God wanted than what He wanted.[5] Jesus knew that God knew what He was doing. He trusted Him and had faith in Him.

Jesus was never trapped by the Roman soldiers. His "capture" was no surprise to Him. He went to Jerusalem knowing He would be killed. Jesus told Pontious Pilate that His purpose on earth was to die, otherwise His servants would have fought to keep Him free.[6] He even spoke of "taking up the cross" well before He was forced to carry one.[7]

So, Jesus came to die. What does that mean to you? What does that do for you? It redeems you. That means you are free. Sin kills.[8] It brings illness and death and destruction. But, you can be free from the punishment because of Jesus' sacrifice. That doesn't mean you can do anything you want. "Why not sin if it is covered already?" That means that when you do mess up, and you will, (We all fall short of the glory of God) Jesus has already picked up the tab. All you have to do is acknowledge that Jesus paid for your sins, repent of them and then try not to sin again.

Repent means to turn around. If you repent of something that means you are sorry that you did it and you turn away from doing it again. Let's say you stole a pack of bubble gum from the

71

store. Then, you feel bad about it and take it back. You apologize to the manager for stealing. You have repented. The next day your friend tries to get you to steal another pack of gum, because no one caught you the first time. You tell him no. It is wrong. You have repented from that behavior. You have turned away from it.

You have been redeemed from the punishment of sin, which is death. Does that mean you will live forever? Yes and no. If you accept Jesus Christ as your Savior you will be given eternal life. But, your body will probably still die (unless Jesus comes back first.) Your spirit, which is what is really you anyway, will live eternally with God.

So... why did Jesus come? He came to die, so that you may live, eternally.

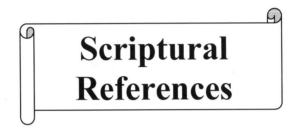

Scriptural References

1 **Pilate therefore said to Him, "Are You a king then?" Jesus answered, "You say rightly that I am a King. For this cause I was born, and for this cause I have come into the world, that I should bear witness to the truth. Everyone who is of the truth hears My voice." John 18:37**

2 **May He grant you according to your heart's desire, And fulfill all your purpose. Psalm 20:4**

3 **And He said to them, "Why did you seek Me? Did you not know that I must be about My Father's business?" Luke 2:49**

4 **For as by one man's disobedience many were made sinners, so also by one Man's obedience many will be made righteous. Romans 5:19**

5 **saying, "Father, if it is Your will, take this cup away from Me; nevertheless not My will, but Yours, be done." Luke 22:42**

6 **Jesus answered, "My kingdom is not of this world. If my kingdom were of this world, My servants would fight, so that I should not be delivered to the Jews; but now My kingdom is not from here." John 18:36**

7 **Then Jesus said to His disciples, "If anyone desires to come after Me, let him deny himself, and take up his cross, and follow Me. Matthew 16:24**

8 **For the wages of sin is death, but the gift of God is eternal life in Christ Jesus our Lord. Romans 6:23**

Discussion Questions

1) What is your God given destiny?
   (Each person has to figure this out for themselves. It takes some people a lifetime.)

2) How do you figure out what God's destiny is for your life?
   (Look at what you are good at and what you enjoy doing. That is a good place to start. Talk to God about it. He will show you His plans for you when the time is right.)

3) Does everyone fulfill God's destiny for their life?
   (Sadly many, many people never even try to figure out what God has planned for them.)

4) Why did Jesus choose to die, if He had a choice?
   (He knew that was God's destiny for Him. Jesus knew how important His sacrifice was to the world.)

5) If you know that your sin is going to be forgiven because all you have to do is repent, why not just commit sin whenever you feel like it and say "sorry" every time?
   (To repent means to turn away from sin. If you have truly repented, you aren't going to turn around and do it again. People who really love God appreciate Jesus' sacrifice. They don't want to sin, because they don't want to cause God sadness.)

Activity

Directions: "Decode" the message.
(Answer to puzzle is scripture of the week: **For this cause I was born, and for this cause I have come into the world, that I should bear witness to the truth. Everyone who is of the truth hears My voice.**" John 18:37)

The Birth of Christ

Lesson Eighteen

Scripture of the Week:
"For there is born to you this day in the city of David a Savior, who is Christ the Lord.

Luke 2:11

Lesson: The donkey walked slowly along with Joseph leading it. Mary and Joseph had been traveling for three days from Nazareth to Bethlehem. "I am getting tired, Joseph. And this baby is really beginning to kick. Do you think we can find a place to stop for the night?"

"Okay, Mary," answered Joseph. He felt bad about having her on that donkey anyway. The baby was supposed to come at just any time. Why did Caesar Augustus choose now to have everybody registered? The city was very crowded with all the people coming in for the census.

Joseph saw a light on a hill. He hoped it was an inn. When they got closer, he saw that it was. He knocked at the door. The innkeeper answered. Joseph asked the man for a room, explaining they were tired from their journey. The innkeeper sadly shook his head, "I am sorry, we are full."

"But, sir," Joseph pleaded. "My wife is with child and she is very tired. We have had a long journey. Please, do you know of anywhere we could go."

The innkeeper had compassion for them. "Because of this census, all of the inns are full. But, I have a stable behind the inn. You are welcome to stay there. At least you will be out of the weather."

"Thank you sir," Joseph said. He then turned to Mary and explained all that the innkeeper told him. They went to the stable and got as comfortable as they could. It was that very night that Mary gave birth to her first born Son. She wrapped Him in swaddling clothes and laid Him in a manger.

In the same country there were many shepherds watching over their flocks. An angel of God came to the shepherds in the night as they worked. It shone so brightly, it scared the men. But, the angel said to them, "Don't be afraid. I bring you good news. Tonight a Savior was born. You will find Him wrapped in swaddling clothes, lying in a manger." Then, suddenly a large group of angels joined the angel in the sky, praising God, saying, "Glory to God in the highest, And on earth peace, goodwill toward men!"

Immediately, the men left the fields and went to Bethlehem. They found Jesus and His mother and Joseph in the stable, just as the angels said they would. After seeing this great sight, they told everyone who would listen about the Christ Child.

When Jesus was old enough, Mary and Joseph took Him into Jerusalem to present Him to the Lord. Simeon, a man in the temple where they brought Jesus, picked up the baby and blessed Him. Then, he said to Mary, "Behold, this Child is destined for the fall and rising of many in Israel, and for a sign which will be spoken against, that the thoughts of many hearts may be revealed."

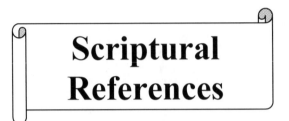

Scriptural References

The entirety of this lesson was taken from Luke, Chapter two.

Discussion Questions

1) Why do you think God made sure that Jesus was born in a stable, instead of in a very nice place?

   (Perhaps God wanted Jesus to come from humble beginnings so people would know that His greatness came from God, instead of from having lots of money and power from the world.)

2) Why did the angel tell a bunch of shepherds in the field about Jesus?

   (God knew that these men would come to see and worship the newborn Jesus. And that they would spread the news of His birth. Again, this is an example of Jesus coming from humble beginnings.)

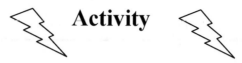# Activity

Directions: Pretend that you are a reporter and you have just visited the Christ Child in the stable. Write a story for your newspaper explaining what you saw and what it means to the world. Don't forget the catchy headline!

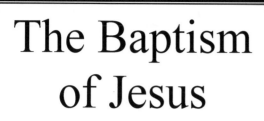

The Baptism of Jesus

Lesson Nineteen

Scripture of the Week:
"Repent for the kingdom of heaven is at hand."

Matthew 3:2

Lesson: When Mary had first found out she was pregnant, she went to visit her cousin Elizabeth. An angel had told Mary that Elizabeth was also pregnant and had been for six months. But, Elizabeth was old and had never been able to have children. This surely had to be a miracle.[1]

When Mary greeted her cousin, Elizabeth's baby, having heard Mary's voice, jumped for joy inside his mother.[2] They both knew they were going to have very special children... both very important to the Kingdom of God. Mary stayed with Elizabeth for three months, then returned home. Shortly after Mary left, Elizabeth gave birth to her baby boy.[3] They named him John, like the angel Gabriel told them to. This was the child, John the Baptist, that Isaiah had prophesied about many, many years before, saying, "The voice of one crying in the wilderness: Prepare the way of the Lord; Make His paths straight."[4]

Many years later, when both John and Jesus had grown up, they met. John had become a rugged, hairy man that traveled the countryside dressed in camel hair and preached about the kingdom of heaven. He spoke of repenting from sins and baptism by water.[5] But, he also spoke of a Man who would come after him, One who was far greater than he, who would baptize with fire. In the meantime, Jesus had grown in wisdom and size. Both men and God looked at Him as an honorable Man.[6] He had spent years learning, but His greatest works were still to come.

John was busy baptizing people in the river Jordan. Then he looked up and saw that Jesus was standing there, waiting to be baptized. John immediately recognized Him as the Son of God and began to protest. "I need to be baptized by You, and You are coming to me?" John knew that He baptized people to repentance and the forgiveness of sins. And he also knew that Jesus was sinless. So, he could not understand why Jesus felt He needed to be baptized.[7]

Jesus answered him, "Allow me to be baptized. It is the right thing to do."[8] Remember that Jesus was to take on the sins of the whole world. Perhaps, He was confessing the sin of the world and repenting of it with this act.

So, John baptized Jesus. And immediately, as He came out of the water, the heavens opened up. The Spirit of God fell upon Him. Then, the voice of God thundered from the sky, "This is My beloved Son, in whom I am well pleased."[9] Jesus was obedient to God and God was very proud of Him. Imagine the reaction of all the people who were waiting in line to be baptized. It was this act of obedience that was the beginning of the ministry of Jesus. Up until this point, there are no recorded miracles performed by Him. But, after His baptism by water and fire His greatest works began.

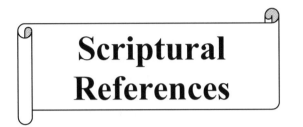

Scriptural References

1 "Now indeed, Elizabeth your relative has also conceived a son in her old age; and this is now the sixth month for her who was called barren. Luke 1:36
   Now Mary arose in those days and went into the hill country with haste, to a city of Judah, and entered the house of Zacharias and greeted Elizabeth. Luke 1:39,40

2 And it happened, when Elizabeth heard the greeting of Mary, that the babe leaped in her womb; and Elizabeth was filled with the Holy Spirit. Luke 1:41

3 Now Elizabeth's full time came for her to be delivered, and she brought forth a son. Luke 1:57

4 as it is written in the book of the words of Isaiah the prophet, saying: "The voice of one crying in the wilderness: 'Prepare the way of the LORD; Make His paths straight. Luke 3:4

5 And John himself was clothed in camel's hair, with a leather belt around his waist; and his food was locusts and wild honey. Then Jerusalem, all Judea, and all the region around the Jordan went out to him and were baptized by him in the Jordan, confessing their sins. Matthew 3:4-6

6 And Jesus increased in wisdom and stature, and in favor with God and men. Luke 2:52

7 Then Jesus came from Galilee to John at the Jordan to be baptized by him. And John tried to prevent Him, saying, "I need to be baptized by You, and You are coming to me?" Matthew 3:13,14

8 But Jesus answered and said to him, "Permit it to be so now, for thus it is fitting for us to fulfill all righteousness." Then he allowed Him. Matthew 3:15

9 When He had been baptized, Jesus came up immediately from the water; and behold, the heavens were opened to Him, and He saw the Spirit of God descending like a dove and alighting upon Him. And suddenly a voice came from heaven, saying, "This is My beloved Son, in whom I am well pleased." Matthew 3:16,17

Discussion Questions

1) Why do you think Mary went to visit her cousin Elizabeth?

(Mary was pregnant, even though she was a virgin. Elizabeth was pregnant, even though she was old. Mary probably realized these were both miracles. And she probably wanted to visit her cousin so they could share these miracles together. If you had a miracle happen to you, and you knew that your cousin did too, you would probably want to talk to your cousin about the miracles you had in common. In addition, there were probably many rumors going around about Mary being pregnant before she was married. She may have wanted to get away from them.)

2) Why do you think God made sure that Jesus and John the Baptist were cousins (albeit not first cousins)?

(There is nothing in the scriptures to give us a clue to this. However, allow the kids to speculate offering these thoughts if they seem "stuck"...

...Perhaps God wanted Mary to have someone "in her boat," so to speak, like her cousin Elizabeth to talk to, so they could support each other.

...Perhaps God wanted someone from Jesus' own bloodline to be the "voice of one crying in the wilderness.")

3) Why was Jesus baptized, if He never sinned?

(He took on the sin of the world. By being baptized, perhaps He was repenting of those sins, even though He did not commit them. He set an example for the world by being baptized.)

4) What does it mean to be baptized with fire?

(Baptism by fire is the baptism of the Holy Spirit. The fire is the fire of God's spirit.)

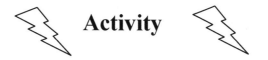

Activity

Directions: Immediately after Jesus was baptized, the Holy Spirit descended on Him like a dove. Draw and color this scene as you imagine it looked.

Temptation by Satan

Lesson Twenty

Scripture of the Week:
Therefore submit to God. Resist the devil and he will flee from you.

James 4:7

Lesson: John had just baptized Jesus. The Holy Spirit had come upon Him and was guiding Him. It guided Him into the wilderness where He fasted for forty days and forty nights. He had no food or drink for all of that time. That, in itself, was a miracle, since man cannot live without water for more than a few days. At the end of this time, He was hungry. It was then that the devil came to tempt Him.

"If You are the Son of God, command that these stones become bread," the devil tested Him. He knew that Jesus was the Son of God and that He could turn stones into bread. He also knew how hungry Jesus must be after forty days without food.

But Jesus resisted him, quoting the word of God, "It is written, 'Man shall not live by bread alone, but by every word that proceeds from the mouth of God.'" Jesus knew that although food was important to the body, spiritual food was more important to the spirit.

Then the devil took Him into the holy city and put Him on the very top of a church building and said to Him, If you are the Son of God, throw Yourself down. For it is written; 'He shall give His angels charge over you,' and 'In their hands they shall bear you up, Lest you dash your foot against a stone.'" Even the devil can quote scripture when it suits him. Although the devil cannot argue with the truth of the word of God, he can twist it to deceive people.

But, Jesus was not worried. He answered simply, "It is written again, 'You shall not tempt the Lord your God,'"

So the devil tried one more time. He took Jesus to the top of a very high mountain, and showed Him all the kingdoms of the world and their glory. And he said to Him, "All these things I will give You if You will fall down and worship me." Even though the earth and all its fullness belong to the Lord, because of the sin of Adam, the devil had become the lord of the earth. The future kingdoms were his to give to Jesus.

But, Jesus was not fooled. He knew about God's plan to take back the world through Jesus' death and resurrection. By this time, Jesus had probably grown bored and annoyed with the devil. He answered him, "Away with you, satan! For it is written, 'You shall worship the Lord your God, and Him only you shall serve.'"

Having been commanded to leave, the devil departed Jesus. He would be back again another day to wage war against Jesus, through other people. Then, angels came and ministered to Jesus. Even Jesus needed to be ministered to after attacks from the devil.

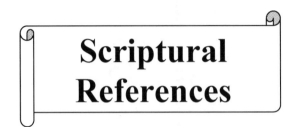

Scriptural References

The entirety of lesson was taken from Matthew, chapter four.

Discussion Questions

1) Why did satan tempt Jesus?

   (If satan could tempt Jesus to sin, Jesus would no longer be a perfect sacrifice for the world. That would mean God's plan for your salvation would not have worked. Although satan didn't really know all this, he knew that to attack God's Son was to attack God.)

2) Why did Jesus go into the wilderness and fast for forty days and nights?

   (The Holy Spirit led Him there to be tempted by the devil. If Jesus was never ever tempted by the devil, people would feel that He could not relate to temptation that is on the earth. Because Jesus has gone through temptation, He can serve as an example to us not to give in to temptation.)

3) Why didn't Jesus just command the stones to become bread, if He was hungry?

   (It would have been a sin to give in to the temptation of satan.)

4) Why did the angels minister to Jesus?

   (After being tempted by the devil, Jesus probably could use a little ministering. We are meant to minister to one another, to help each other. That is one of the reasons that we go to church.)

 **Activity**

Directions: Fill in the blanks. You will find what you should do when the devil tempts you. (Teacher Note: The answer is in the scripture of the week.)

1) How many days did Jesus fast? <u>forty</u>
2) Satan tried to get Jesus to turn the stones into <u>bread.</u>
3) Who led Jesus into the wilderness? <u>Holy Spirit</u>
4) What caused the devil to have control of the kingdoms of the world? <u>sin</u>
5) <u>Angels</u> came to minister to Jesus after the devil left.
6) Jesus answered the devil by quoting <u>scripture</u>.

When the devil tempts you, you should **<u>resist</u>** him.

Jesus Come to Town

Lesson Twenty-One

Scripture of the Week:

Tell the daughter of Zion, 'Behold your King is coming to you, Lowly, and sitting on a donkey, A colt, the foal of a donkey.'"

Matthew 21:5

Lesson: It was a cool, sunny morning. Passover was just a few days away. Jesus and His disciples were just outside the village of Bethany. The disciples thought they were going into Jerusalem to celebrate the Passover feast. But, Jesus knew the real reason He was there. He was there to die.

After breakfast, Jesus sent two of His disciples into a nearby village. He told them, "As soon as you enter the village, you will see the colt of a donkey tied up. Bring it to me. If anyone asks you, tell them it is for the Lord and they will let you have it." [1]

So, the men went into the village and found the colt, just as Jesus said. But, the people saw them untying the colt and asked them what they were doing. The disciples told them, "The Lord has need of it." So, they let them have it. Word quickly spread throughout the villages that Jesus was coming to town.

The disciples brought the donkey to Jesus. They put their clothes on the donkey's back, and helped Jesus on it. The slow ride into Jerusalem began. By the time Jesus came down the hill, the townspeople had made a path for him. They had spread out their clothes and palm branches all over the path, to honor Him. [2] That is why the Sunday before Easter is called "Palm Sunday," to celebrate Jesus' triumphant entrance into Jerusalem.

The people were so excited to see Jesus, they cried out, "Hosanna to the Son of David! Blessed is He who comes in the name of the Lord! Hosanna in the highest!" [3]

The chief priests and the scribes were angry and jealous. They didn't like the idea of Jesus getting all the attention. They told Him to tell the crowd to be quiet.

But Jesus replied, "If they were quiet, the very stones would cry out in praise." [4] Jesus knew that He was the Son of God. And He knew that by honoring Him, the people were also honoring God.

Jesus looked on the beautiful city, then wept. He was very sad. He knew that soon the whole city would be destroyed and all the people within it, because Jerusalem did not recognize the day that God came to save it. [5] (Some thirty-seven years later, in AD 70, the Romans did destroy Jerusalem.)

Jesus and His disciples spent the night at their friends', Mary, Martha, and Lazarus, house in Bethany. The following morning, a Monday, Jesus went back into Jerusalem. This time, He went into the temple. It was once again filled with moneychangers and traders.

Many people came into Jerusalem to worship. While they were there, they often sacrificed animals for forgiveness of sins. Remember that this was before Jesus became the ultimate sacrifice and changed things forever. Because people came from many different places, they had different types of money. So, merchants set up businesses to exchange money and sell animals to be sacrificed. These moneychangers and traders became greedier and greedier, trying to take advantage of all the people coming in for the Passover Feast. And they got closer and closer to the temple doors, until, finally, they just moved into the temple and took it over.

Jesus had cleared out the temple once before. Today He was filled with righteous anger. He turned over their tables, as He spoke God's word, "It is written, that God's House shall be a house of prayer for all nations; but you have made it into a den of thieves." [6]

Once Jesus had cleared the temple, He began teaching and healing in it once again. [7] The people hung on His every word. This made the chief priests and the scribes very mad. So, they tried to figure out a way to destroy Jesus and His works, once and for all.

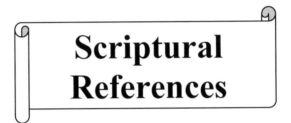

Scriptural References

1   **Saying to them, "Go into the village opposite you, and immediately you will find a donkey tied, and a colt with her. Loose them and bring them to Me. "And if anyone says anything to you, you shall say, 'The Lord has need of them,' and immediately he will send them." Matthew 21:2,3**

2   **So the disciples went and did as Jesus commanded them. They brought the donkey and the colt, laid their clothes on them, and set Him on them. And a very great multitude spread their clothes on the road; others cut down branches from the trees and spread them on the road. Matthew 21:6-8**

3   **Then the multitudes who went before and those who followed cried out, saying: "Hosanna to the Son of David! 'Blessed is He who comes in the name of the Lord!' Hosanna in the highest!" Matthew 21:9**

4   **But He answered and said to them, "I tell you that if these should keep silent, the stones would immediately cry out." Luke 19:40**

5   **Now as He drew near, He saw the city and wept over it, saying, "If you had known, even you, especially in this your day, the things that make for your peace! But now they are hidden from your eyes. "For days will come upon you when your enemies**

will build an embankment around you, surround you and close you in on every side, and level you, and your children within you, to the ground; and they will not leave in you one stone upon another, because you did not know the time of your visitation." Luke 19:41-44

6 Then Jesus went into the temple of God and drove out all those who bought and sold in the temple, and overturned the tables of the moneychangers and the seats of those who sold doves. And He said to them, "It is written, 'My house shall be called a house of prayer,' but you have made it a 'den of thieves.' " Matthew 21:12,13

7 Then the blind and the lame came to Him in the temple, and He healed them. Matthew 21:14

Discussion Questions

1) Why did Jesus go into Jerusalem if He knew He would be killed?
   (Jesus knew it was God's plan for Him to die in Jerusalem and that the time had come.)

2) Jesus was mad because the moneychangers and merchants had taken over the temple. He flipped over their tables. Was this the same Jesus that is called the Prince of Peace? Was it okay for Jesus to get mad and start knocking things over?
   (Jesus was filled with what is called "righteous anger." That means that He had every right to be mad. Evil, greedy people had turned the house of God, which is supposed to be a house of prayer for the world, into a "den of thieves." Jesus said that He did not come to bring peace, but a sword **(Matthew 10:34)**. Jesus stands against evil, whatever form it takes.)

3) When Jesus came into Jerusalem the people cheered Him. But, just a few days later, the same crowds yelled for Him to be crucified. What happened?
   (The chief priests and the elders of the church convinced the people that Jesus was a liar. They talked them into asking for Barabbas, the murderer to be released and for Jesus to be destroyed.)

4) Why did the leaders of the church, who were supposed to be God's people, convince everyone to kill Jesus?
   (They were mad at Him for spending time with the lost sinners, instead of spending time with them, telling them how "great" they are. They were also jealous of the attention Jesus received. And Jesus was not the image of what many of them believed the Savior should be.)

Activity

Have the class act out the events in this lesson... from retrieving the donkey to healing in the temple.

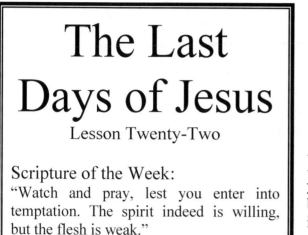

The Last Days of Jesus

Lesson Twenty-Two

Scripture of the Week:
"Watch and pray, lest you enter into temptation. The spirit indeed is willing, but the flesh is weak."

Matthew 26:41

Lesson: Jesus knew He was going to die, yet He went willingly into Jerusalem. It had been a busy week. He had spent a lot of time in the temple teaching and healing. Everyone who heard Him was amazed. People couldn't wait to get a chance to get into the temple and have Jesus lay His hands on them. But the scribes and the Pharisees couldn't wait to get their hands on Jesus. They were jealous and wanted to destroy Him. So, they enlisted the help of one of Jesus' own. [1]

Thursday night Jesus gathered together with His disciples for a special Passover dinner. He knew it would be His last. And He also knew He was about to be betrayed. [2]

As He broke the bread with His disciples, He gave thanks and then told them, "This is My body which is given for you. Whenever you do this, do this in remembrance of Me." The disciples were a little confused. But they were used to Jesus speaking in riddles to them. Then, after dinner, He gave wine to the men. And He said, "This is My blood of the new covenant, shed for many." [3]

Then, Jesus told the men that He was about to be betrayed by one of them. They all wanted to know who would do such a thing, except Judas. He had already been to the chief priests. He had promised to hand Jesus over to them, for a price. And tonight would be the night.

After dinner, Jesus went to the Garden of Gethsemane to pray. He took Peter, James, and John with Him and asked them to watch and to pray. Jesus went off by Himself to talk to His Dad. "Father," He prayed, "everything is possible with You. If there is another way, please let it be another way. But, if this is Your will, then so be it." [4] He was very sad. He knew His time to die had come. He went to check on Peter, James, and John. They were sleeping. Jesus was a little annoyed with them. "Couldn't you stay awake for one hour?" [5] They didn't know what to say. Jesus went back to pray again. And again He asked God, if there was any other way... [6] He returned to His disciples, who were sleeping again. [7] Jesus told them again to pray, then He went back to pray some more. Jesus prayed so hard that sweat dripped off him like blood. Then, He returned to His disciples who were asleep yet again and woke them. "The hour has come. See, here comes My betrayer." [8]

Judas was walking toward Jesus, with a multitude of people carrying lanterns, torches, and weapons. They were the troops given to him by the scribes to "capture" Jesus. Judas kissed

Jesus. [9] Jesus spoke, "Judas, are you betraying Me with a kiss?" [10] Jesus knew that Judas had kissed Him, so that the troops would know which one Jesus was. When Simon Peter, one of the disciples, realized what was happening, he drew his sword and cut off the ear of the high priest's servant. [11] Much to everyone's surprise, Jesus scolded Peter, "Put away your sword. If you live by the sword, you will die by the sword. Don't you realize that all I would have to do is ask God and He would give me twelve legions of angels this very minute to protect Me? [12] But, that is not how it is supposed to be." Then, Jesus touched the man's ear and said, "Permit even this," and it was healed. [13] The men took hold of Jesus. And Jesus' disciples ran away.

Judas was paid thirty silver pieces for delivering Jesus to those who wanted Him dead. [14]

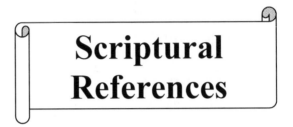

Scriptural References

1   Then one of the twelve, called Judas Iscariot, went to the chief priests and said, "What are you willing to give me if I deliver Him to you?" And they counted out to him thirty pieces of silver.   Matthew 26:14,15

2   Now as they were eating, He said, "Assuredly, I say to you, one of you will betray Me."   Matthew 26:21

3   And as they were eating, Jesus took bread, blessed and broke *it*, and gave *it* to them and said, "Take, eat; this is My body." And He said to them, "This is My blood of the new covenant, which is shed for many.   Mark 14:22,24

4   He went a little farther and fell on His face, and prayed, saying, "O My Father, if it is possible, let this cup pass from Me; nevertheless, not as I will, but as You will." Matthew 26:39

5   Then He came to the disciples and found them asleep, and said to Peter, "What? Could you not watch with Me one hour?   Matthew 26:40

6   Again, a second time, He went away and prayed, saying, "O My Father, if this cup cannot pass away from Me unless I drink it, Your will be done." Matthew 26:42

7   And He came and found them asleep again, for their eyes were heavy. Matthew 26:43

8   Then He came to His disciples and said to them, "Are *you* still sleeping and resting? Behold, the hour is at hand, and the Son of Man is being betrayed into the hands of sinners. "Rise, let us be going. See, My betrayer is at hand."

Matthew 26:45,46

9 And while He was still speaking, behold, Judas, one of the twelve, with a great multitude with swords and clubs, came from the chief priests and elders of the people. Now His betrayer had given them a sign, saying, "Whomever I kiss, He is the One; seize Him." Immediately he went up to Jesus and said, "Greetings, Rabbi!" and kissed Him. **Matthew 26:47,48,49**

10 But Jesus said to him, "Judas, are you betraying the Son of Man with a kiss?" **Luke 22:48**

11 And suddenly, one of those who were with Jesus stretched out his hand and drew his sword, struck the servant of the high priest, and cut off his ear. **Matthew 26:51**

12 But Jesus said to him, "Put your sword in its place, for all who take the sword will perish by the sword. Or do you think that I cannot now pray to My Father, and He will provide Me with more than twelve legions of angels? **Matthew 26:52,53**

13 But Jesus answered and said, "Permit even this." And He touched his ear and healed him. **Luke 22:51**

14 and said, "What are you willing to give me if I deliver Him to you?" And they counted out to him thirty pieces of silver. **Matthew 26:15**

Discussion Questions

1) Why did Judas betray Jesus?

   (Judas was paid thirty silver pieces to betray Jesus. But, he also had satan in him.) **Now, after the piece of bread, satan entered him. Then Jesus said to him, "What you do, do quickly." John 13:27**

2) When Peter realized what was about to happen, he drew his sword and cut off a man's ear, in defense of Jesus. But, Jesus got upset with Peter about it. Why?

   (Jesus knew that this way the way it had to be, even though Peter didn't understand that. Jesus explained to Peter that those who live by the sword die by the sword.)

3) In the garden of Gethsemane, Jesus prayed to God three times, asking Him "If there is another way, please let it be another way." Jesus didn't want to suffer and die. But, He told God, "Let it be Your way." Did God answer Jesus' prayer?

(God answered Jesus' prayer. But, the answer was "No." Jesus could have just asked God not to allow it to happen and it wouldn't have. But, instead, He prayed... "If there is another way, so be it. Nevertheless, let it be Your way, not My way. But, this was the only way.)

4) If God can do anything, why did Jesus have to die? Why couldn't it have worked out a different way?

(The Bible is made up of two parts, the Old Testament and the New Testament. A testament is an "agreement, a covenant, a promise." You may have heard of someone's "last will and testament." A person can write their last will and testament whenever they want. But, nothing is done about it until that person dies. Jesus' will and testament was to give us the Kingdom of God and the promise of eternal life. But, in order for it to work for us, Jesus had to die. If His earthly body did not die, no one could "inherit" the Kingdom of God and eternal life. You can't inherit anything until the person giving it to you dies.)

(For where there is a testament, there must also of necessity be the death of the testator. For a testament is in force after men are dead, since it has no power at all while the testator lives. Hebrews 9:16,17)

 **Activity**

Directions: Draw and color a picture of something that happened during the last days of Jesus (last supper, praying in the garden, the crowd coming to get Jesus, Jesus healing the man's ear, etc.)

The Resurrection

Lesson Twenty-Three

Scripture of the Week:
"But when you give a feast, invite the poor, the maimed, the lame, the blind. "And you will be blessed, because they cannot repay you; for you shall be repaid at the resurrection of the just."

Luke 14: 13,14

Lesson: Friday morning came. Jesus had been beaten and thrown into prison. But, the worst had just begun. They took Him to see the governor, Pontius Pilate. Lots of people testified against Jesus before the governor. Most of what they said was lies. But, they did tell Pilate that Jesus had called Himself the King of the Jews. So Pilate asked Jesus, "Are you the King of the Jews?" Jesus answered, "It is as you say." [1] Pilate knew the Pharisees were out to destroy Jesus because they were jealous of Him. [2] Besides, Pilate's own wife warned him not to have anything to do with the plot to destroy Jesus, because she had had a dream about Jesus that haunted her. [3] So, Pilate looked for a way out. Then he remembered one of the people saying Jesus had been teaching in Galilee. Ah, finally, a way out. He sent Jesus to Galilee, to be judged by the Galilean governor, Herod. [4]

Herod was excited to inherit Jesus. He had heard about Jesus' teachings and great miracles. Herod was hoping to witness a miracle himself. But, when he started questioning Jesus, with the angry scribes and Pharisees standing by, Jesus wouldn't say a word in His own defense. This made Herod mad. He must have been embarrassed to be ignored in front of all those other people, him being the governor and ruler of Galilee. So, he made fun of Jesus, dressing Him in a royal robe. But, they knew that Jesus had done nothing wrong, so they returned Him to Pilate. [5]

Now, Jesus had become Pilate's problem again. Pilate went to the chief priests and the people and told them, "I have found that Jesus has done nothing wrong, so I will chastise Him and release Him." [6] Pilate knew that the custom was to release one prisoner during Passover. Surely the crowds would choose Jesus, an innocent Man. Then, he could be out of this difficult position once and for all.

But, the chief priests and the Pharisees had already thought of that. They told the people they needed to get rid of that troublemaker, Jesus. The crowd fell for the lies, and called for a murderer, Barrabas, to be released instead of Jesus. [7]

Pilate was worried. He knew it was wrong to kill Jesus, but he was afraid of the crowd that was growing more and more angry. They started shouting, "Crucify Him! Crucify Him!" Pilate wrote the title "Jesus of Nazareth, The King of the Jews" and had them put it on the cross. Then he released Jesus to the Roman soldiers, and washed his hands to show that he was not the one killing an innocent man. [8]

The soldiers dressed up Jesus in a purple robe and put a crown of thorns on His head. Then they hit Him and spit at Him and pretended to worship Him on one knee. They laughed as the blood trickled down His face. They beat Him until it was hard to recognize Him as Jesus. Then they ripped off the robe and put His clothes back on Him. [9] That is when they gave Jesus a cross to carry. He was only able to carry it a short way, because He was so weak after His beating. So, the soldiers picked a man out of the crowd to carry it the rest of the way. [10] This man, Simon, had come to Jerusalem with his two young sons to celebrate Passover. When they reached Golgotha, "the place of the skull", the soldiers ripped off Jesus' clothes again, then nailed His hands and feet to a cross and stood the cross upright. [11] There were criminals on both sides of Him, being killed for crimes they had committed. [12]

He was there for hours. But in His final moments He cried out to God, "My God, My God, why have You forsaken Me?" [13] For the first time in His life, He did not feel God's presence with Him. By hanging on that cross, paying the price for every sin ever committed and every sin that would ever be committed, Jesus took on the sin of the world. And God had to turn His back on that sin. Then Jesus cried out again, "It is finished!" and He died. [14]

At that moment, the earth quaked, the sun darkened, the rocks split, and the veil of the temple was torn in two. Graves opened up and lots of God's people came out of them, as if they had only been asleep all this time, instead of dead. [15]

A rich man named Joseph went to Pontius Pilate and asked if he could have Jesus' body to bury. Pilate gave it to him. So Joseph had Jesus' body wrapped in cloth and put inside a new tomb that had been dug out of a rock. [16]

The chief priests and the Pharisees remembered how Jesus told everyone that on the third day He would rise again. So, they went to Pilate and asked him to secure the tomb, so that none of Jesus' followers would steal His body and say He rose from the dead. Pilate gave them permission to secure the tomb. The Pharisees sealed the tomb with a giant stone and put two guards outside it. They were going to stay for three days, to make sure no one messed with the tomb. [17]

But, on that Sunday, while Mary, the mother of Jesus, and Mary Magdalene came to anoint the body of Jesus; they heard a great earthquake. An angel appeared to them. The guards shook with fear and passed out. The women were afraid too. But, the angel spoke to them. "Don't be afraid. I know you are looking for Jesus. But, He isn't here. Come inside and take a look. He has risen, just like He said He would." The women quickly ran into the tomb and found... nothing but the burial clothes. The angel told them, "Go tell His disciples that He is risen. He is on His way to Galilee." [18]

The women were so excited, they ran to find His disciples. But, on their way, they ran into Jesus. It was true. He is alive! Jesus spoke to them. "Rejoice! Do not be afraid. Go and tell My brethren to go to Galilee, and there they will see Me." [19]

When the tomb guards came to their senses, they ran to the chief priests and told them about what had happened. They knew this meant trouble. So the priests paid the guards to tell everyone that Jesus' disciples stole His body as they slept. This story is still told among the Jews today. [20]

But, Jesus walked the earth another forty days, and instructed His disciples to "Go into all the world and preach the gospel to every creature." [21] Then, He rose up into heaven and sat down at the right hand of God. All authority has been given to Jesus in heaven and on earth. [22]

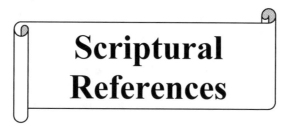

Scriptural References

1   Now Jesus stood before the governor. And the governor asked Him, saying, "Are You the King of the Jews?" So Jesus said to him, "It is as you say." And while He was being accused by the chief priests and elders, He answered nothing.   Matthew 27:11,12

2   For he knew that they had handed Him over because of envy.   Matthew 27:18

3   While he was sitting on the judgment seat, his wife sent to him, saying, "Have nothing to do with that just Man, for I have suffered many things today in a dream because of Him." Matthew 27:19

4   And as soon as he knew that He belonged to Herod's jurisdiction, he sent Him to Herod, who was also in Jerusalem at that time.   Luke 23:7

5   Now when Herod saw Jesus, he was exceedingly glad; for he had desired for a long time to see Him, because he had heard many things about Him, and he hoped to see some miracle done by Him. Then he questioned Him with many words, but He answered him nothing. And the chief priests and scribes stood and vehemently accused Him. Then Herod, with his men of war, treated Him with contempt and mocked Him, arrayed Him in a gorgeous robe, and sent Him back to Pilate. Luke 23:8-11

6   said to them, "You have brought this Man to me, as one who misleads the people. And indeed, having examined Him in your presence, I have found no fault in this Man concerning those things of which you accuse Him; "I will therefore chastise Him and release Him" Luke 23:14,16

7   But the chief priests and elders persuaded the multitudes that they should ask for Barabbas and destroy Jesus. Matthew 27:20

8 Pilate said to them, "What then shall I do with Jesus who is called Christ?" They all said to him, "Let Him be crucified!" Then the governor said, "Why, what evil has He done?" But they cried out all the more, saying, "Let Him be crucified!" When Pilate saw that he could not prevail at all, but rather that a tumult was rising, he took water and washed his hands before the multitude, saying, "I am innocent of the blood of this just Person. You see to it."   Matthew 27:22-24

9 Then the soldiers of the governor took Jesus into the Praetorium and gathered the whole garrison around Him. And they stripped Him and put a scarlet robe on Him. When they had twisted a crown of thorns, they put it on His head, and a reed in His right hand. And they bowed the knee before Him and mocked Him, saying, "Hail, King of the Jews!" Then they spat on Him, and took the reed and struck Him on the head. And when they had mocked Him, they took the robe off Him, put His own clothes on Him, and led Him away to be crucified.   Matthew 27:27-31

10 Now as they came out, they found a man of Cyrene, Simon by name.   Him they compelled to bear His cross.   Matthew 27:32

11 Then they crucified Him, and divided His garments, casting lots, that it might be fulfilled which was spoken by the prophet: "They divided My garments among them, And for My clothing they cast lots."   Matthew 27:35

12 Then two robbers were crucified with Him, one on the right and another on the left. Matthew 27:38

13 And about the ninth hour Jesus cried out with a loud voice, saying, "Eli, Eli, lama sabachthani?" that is, "My God, My God, why have You forsaken Me?"   Matthew 27:46

14 So when Jesus had received the sour wine, He said, "It is finished!" And bowing His head, He gave up His spirit.   John 19:30

15 Then, behold, the veil of the temple was torn in two from top to bottom; and the earth quaked, and the rocks were split, and the graves were opened; and many bodies of the saints who had fallen asleep were raised; and coming out of the graves after His resurrection, they went into the holy city and appeared to many. Matthew 27:51-53

16 Now when evening had come, there came a rich man from Arimathea, named Joseph, who himself had also become a disciple of Jesus. This man went to Pilate and asked for the body of Jesus. Then Pilate commanded the body to be given to him. When Joseph had taken the body, he wrapped it in a clean linen cloth, and laid it in his new tomb which he had hewn out of the rock; and he rolled a large stone against the door of the tomb, and departed. Matthew 27:57-60

17 "Therefore command that the tomb be made secure until the third day, lest His disciples come by night and steal Him away, and say to the people, 'He has risen from the dead.' So the last deception will be worse than the first."   Matthew 27:64

18 Now after the Sabbath, as the first day of the week began to dawn, Mary Magdalene and the other Mary came to see the tomb. And behold, there was a great earthquake; for an angel of the Lord descended from heaven, and came and rolled back the stone from the door, and sat on it. His countenance was like lightning, and his clothing as white as snow. And the guards shook for fear of him, and became like dead men. But the angel answered and said to the women, "Do not be afraid, for I know that you seek Jesus who was crucified. "He is not here; for He is risen, as He said. Come, see the place where the Lord lay. "And go quickly and tell His disciples that He is risen from the dead, and indeed He is going before you into Galilee; there you will see Him. Behold, I have told you." So they went out quickly from the tomb with fear and great joy, and ran to bring His disciples word.   Matthew 28:1-8

19 And as they went to tell His disciples, behold, Jesus met them, saying, "Rejoice!" So they came and held Him by the feet and worshipped Him. Then Jesus said to them, "Do not be afraid. Go and tell My brethren to go to Galilee, and there they will see Me." Matthew 28:9,10

20 Now while they were going, behold, some of the guard came into the city and reported to the chief priests all the things that had happened. When they had assembled with the elders and consulted together, they gave a large sum of money to the soldiers, saying, "Tell them, 'His disciples came at night and stole Him away while we slept.' "And if this comes to the governor's ears, we will appease him and make you secure." So they took the money and did as they were instructed; and this saying is commonly reported among the Jews until this day.   Matthew 28:11-15

21 And He said to them, "Go into all the world and preach the gospel to every creature. Mark 16:15

22 And Jesus came and spoke to them, saying, "All authority has been given to Me in heaven and on earth.   Matthew 28:18

Discussion Questions

1) As the governors questioned Jesus, He remained silent for the most part. Why didn't He speak on His own behalf?

    (Jesus was filled with the Holy Spirit, which probably prompted Him to keep quiet. But, if Jesus had spoke in His own defense, He may have talked His way out of being crucified. Since His death was God's plan, He did not want to do anything against it.)

2) Pontius Pilate was afraid. He knew that Jesus was an innocent man. Even Pilate's wife warned him not to do anything to Jesus because of dreams she had the night before. Why did Pilate agree to let Jesus be crucified?

    (Pilate was more afraid of the angry crowds.)

3) When the Roman soldiers told the chief priests about how Jesus' raised from the dead, then they heard the stories about Jesus and many others who had died, walking around talking to people, what do you think that they thought?

4) Why do you think that Jesus stayed on the earth for another forty days after He had risen from the dead, before He ascended into heaven?

    (Even His disciples doubted when they heard that Jesus had come back to life. Jesus needed them to be convinced, because they were the first ones responsible to spread the gospel throughout the world. It is now the responsibility of all of Jesus' followers, including you.)

Activity

Directions: Draw and color a picture of something in this lesson
(Jesus being tried, Jesus carrying the cross, Jesus on the cross, Jesus rising from the grave, Mary and Mary Magdalene finding the empty tomb, etc.)

Jesus Sends The Holy Spirit

Lesson Twenty-Four

Scripture of the Week:

And I will pray the Father, and He will give you another Helper, that He may abide with your forever

John 14:16

Lesson: Before Jesus left His disciples to join His Father in heaven, He told them that He would send a Helper to be with them. [1] His disciples had been so busy wondering where Jesus was going to really question Him about this Helper.

But, like Jesus always does, He fulfilled His promise to the world. God sent the Holy Spirit to live with men once Jesus went to heaven. The Holy Spirit, sometimes called the Holy Ghost, was sent to teach God's people and to remind His disciples of everything Jesus had said to them. [2] This is how God wrote the Bible. The Holy Spirit whispered God's words into the hearts of those God trusted to write them down. [3]

It was through the Holy Spirit that Christ worked miracles. Jesus told His followers that they would do even greater works than He did with the help of the Holy Spirit. [4] The Spirit dwells in many of Christ's followers today, and performs miracles through them.

The Holy Spirit was given to all of God's children. Any believer who wants can have the Holy Spirit live in them. All they have to do is ask God, in the name of Jesus, for the Holy Spirit. [5] So, what happens if you ask the Holy Spirit to live in you? Does He take over?

No. The Holy Spirit becomes the loving voice of God that speaks to your heart. God always allows you free will. But, with the Holy Spirit living in you, God will guide you in your decisions. [6] Remember, the Holy Spirit, Jesus, and God are one. So, you get Three for the price of One. So, what is that price? Faith. You must believe He is actually with you.

How can you tell for sure that you have been baptized by the Holy Spirit? Will you feel different? Maybe. Maybe not. But, you will now have the ability to pray in tongues. [7] Remember the Holy Spirit does not take over. He will not force the language of angels to come out of your mouth. You can be baptized with the Holy Spirit, and never speak in tongues, if you choose not to. There is a lot of power in it, as you will learn about later. [8] But, it is not forced on you. Once you are baptized, you can open your mouth and start speaking, and it will just come on out. You have to make the sound, but the Holy Spirit puts the words there.

So, you have asked the Holy Spirit into your heart and you believe He is there. What's next? What does this do for you? How do you change?

It becomes a little easier to follow Jesus' example. Because, you have Him inside you, guiding you. He helps make those tough decisions and even the easier ones. He teaches you. He makes the Bible easier to understand. He may even work miracles through you. And suddenly, you are thinking a little more like Jesus. You think about what He would do in a situation, instead of just reacting like you normally do to things. But, you have to learn the sound of His voice to know when it is Him. [9] God speaks to you in a quiet, still voice, most of the time. He speaks to your heart.

What?! What does that mean? Do you actually hear God speak words out loud? Not usually. Most of the time God speaks to us through thoughts and feelings that we have. Have you ever been about to do something that you really shouldn't, but then you get this feeling...? That is probably God.

So how do you know when it is the Holy Spirit and not just your own thoughts, or the devil? After a while you will be able to recognize His voice. [10] You will have a thought or a feeling and you will know that it came from God. But, in the meantime, you can always test it and see if it "lines up with the word." If it agrees with what the Bible says, you can relax and know what you are doing is right. But, if it doesn't, watch out! It may be a trick of the devil. Even after you get to know God's voice, you could be fooled once in a while. [11] So, remember, when you are in doubt; check it out... the Bible that is.

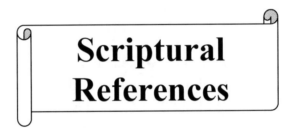

Scriptural References

1 **"And I will pray the Father, and He will give you another Helper, that He may abide with you forever— John 14:16**

2 **"But the Helper, the Holy Spirit, whom the Father will send in My name, He will teach you all things, and bring to your remembrance all things that I said to you. John 14:26**

3 **All Scripture is given by inspiration of God, and is profitable for doctrine, for reproof, for correction, for instruction in righteousness, 2 Timothy 3:16**

4 **"Most assuredly, I say to you, he who believes in Me, the works that I do he will do also; and greater works than these he will do, because I go to My Father. John 14:12**

5 **"If you then, being evil, know how to give good gifts to your children, how much more will your heavenly Father give the Holy Spirit to those who ask Him!" Luke 11:13**

6 "However, when He, the Spirit of truth, has come, He will guide you into all truth; for He will not speak on His own authority, but whatever He hears He will speak; and He will tell you things to come.   John 16:13

7 "And these signs will follow those who believe: In My name they will cast out demons; they will speak with new tongues; Mark 16:17

8 "Behold, I send the Promise of My Father upon you; but tarry in the city of Jerusalem until you are endued with power from on high." Luke 24:49

9 "My sheep hear My voice, and I know them, and they follow Me. John 10:27

10 Pilate therefore said to Him, "Are You a king then?" Jesus answered, "You say rightly that I am a king. For this cause I was born, and for this cause I have come into the world, that I should bear witness to the truth. Everyone who is of the truth hears My voice." John 18:37

11 "For false christs and false prophets will rise and show great signs and wonders to deceive, if possible, even the elect. Matthew 24:24

Discussion Questions

1) Jesus told His followers that they would do even greater works than He did through the Holy Spirit. But, many people are suspicious of healers, prophets, and miracle workers. How do you know if it is the real thing or not?

   (First, check it against the Bible. If it contradicts the Bible, it is not from God. God will never go against His own word. Next, look at the person who is performing the healing, working the miracle, or speaking the prophecy. Do they give the glory and all the credit to God? If they speak and act as if they are doing it all, they probably are... and you can be certain it isn't a true healing, prophecy, or miracle.)

2) How long will the Holy Spirit stay with us?
   (He will stay forever.)

And I will pray the Father, and He will give you another Helper, that He may abide with you forever- John 14:16

3) How have people received the Holy Spirit?

   (In many cases in the Bible, it just came upon them. Some people were prayed over, with hands laid on them, and received. Still others simply asked for it. John the Baptist was filled with the Holy Spirit when his mother was still pregnant with him!)

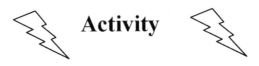

Activity

Directions: Think back over your life. Have you ever had a very strong feeling that you believe may have been from the Holy Spirit. Describe the event (or events) where you believe you heard from God... where He used the Holy Spirit to teach, warn, guide, or communicate with you.

Jesus Rules And Reigns

Lesson Twenty-Five

Scripture of the Week:
For by Him all things were created that are in heaven and that are on earth, visible and invisible, whether thrones or dominions or principalities or powers. All things were created through Him and for Him.

Colossians 1:16

Lesson: So now what is Jesus up to? Last we heard, He had risen from the dead and joined God up in heaven. He said He had to prepare a place for us all. Heaven is full of mansions. [1] They created the earth and everything in it in six days, how long could a few mansions take Jesus? What else is He doing? Is He just hanging out, glad to be there? He isn't doing much, just being worshipped all the time, right? Sure, if you call ruling and reigning over the universe not doing much. [2]

We are all down here on earth, battling satan and his demons all day. So what is Jesus doing? Sitting back, waiting for His enemies to be made His footstool. [3] Hey, wait a minute! Why isn't Jesus helping us out down here? He already did. Jesus is done fighting the forces of evil. He beat them. Made them look real stupid. [4] But, He didn't just kick 'em and take names, then abandon us. He put us in charge of reminding the devil and his demons that they are losers. With His name, we have authority over them. [5] That means, whenever they start trying to mess with our lives, all we have to do is whip out our super-powerful, demon destroying weapons... the name of Jesus and praise. And we have the Holy Spirit in the middle of it all with us, not to mention the angels. We have all that we need.

Jesus gave us those weapons and the job of punishing the devil as a little reward. Think about it. The devil messes with your life, trying to steal and destroy your dreams. But, the joke is on him. You start praising God and crushing satan at the same time. [6]

So, while we are busy crushing satan, Jesus is busy working as King of kings. He keeps track of everything that's going on... in governments, [7] in nature, [8] in your life. He takes care of all the big things and all the little things. He is our High Priest and He prays for us. [9] Don't forget, He even bothers to know what your heart's desire is... and if you follow Him, He may just lead you right into getting it. [10]

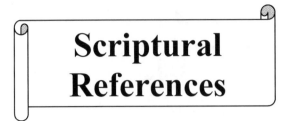

Scriptural References

1   "In My Father's house are many mansions; if it were not so, I would have told you. I go to prepare a place for you. And if I go and prepare a place for you, I will come again and receive you to Myself; that where I am, there you may be also.   John 14:2,3

2   And Jesus came and spoke to them, saying, "All authority has been given to Me in heaven and on earth. Matthew 28:18

3   The LORD said to my Lord, "Sit at My right hand, Till I make Your enemies Your footstool." Psalm 110:1

4   Having disarmed principalities and powers, He made a public spectacle of them, triumphing over them in it.   Colossians 2:15

5   Through You we will push down our enemies; Through Your name we will trample those who rise up against us. Psalm 44:5
    "Behold, I give you the authority to trample on serpents and scorpions, and over all the power of the enemy, and nothing shall by any means hurt you. Luke 10:19

6   Out of the mouth of babes and nursing infants You have ordained strength, Because of Your enemies, That You may silence the enemy and the avenger.
Psalm 8:2

7   Let every soul be subject to the governing authorities. For there is no authority except from God, and the authorities that exist are appointed by God.
Romans 13:1

8   You visit the earth and water it, You greatly enrich it; The river of God is full of water; You provide their grain, For so You have prepared it. You water its ridges abundantly, You settle its furrows; You make it soft with showers, You bless its growth. Psalm 65:9,10

9   Therefore, in all things He had to be made like His brethren, that He might be a merciful and faithful High Priest in things pertaining to God, to make propitiation for the sins of the people. Hebrews 2:17

10 Delight yourself also in the LORD, And He shall give you the desires of your heart. Psalm 37:4

Discussion Questions

1) What is the worst thing we can do to the devil?

(Praise God. It stops him dead in his tracks. He can't stand the presence of God. Since God inhabits the praises of His people. That means if you are praising God, He is right there in the middle of it. And the devil goes running.)

2) What is the worst thing the devil can do to us?

(He tries to destroy our faith in God. If he can do that, God can't do much to help us. Remember the promises of God work only if we have faith in Him. But, if you have your faith in God, nothing that the devil does can destroy you.)

3) Does Jesus really reign on the earth? Does He decide who the president is going to be?
(He sure does.)

Let every soul be subject to the governing authorities. For there is no authority except from God, and the authorities that exist are appointed by God. Romans 13:1

Activity

Directions: Draw and color a picture of Jesus on His throne, ruling the universe

When Jesus Returns

Lesson Twenty-Six

Scripture of the Week:
"Watch therefore, for you know neither the day nor the hour in which the Son of Man is coming."

Matthew 25:13

Lesson: When Jesus left the earth, He told His disciples that He would be back. "When Lord? When will You return?" they wanted to know. But, He told them that no one knew, except for God, the Father. Even Jesus, Himself, did not know. [1] He did tell them some of the signs to watch for, so they would know when it was getting close.

"You will hear about wars and rumors of wars," Jesus explained. "But, don't worry, that won't be the end yet. That has to happen. There will be famines, and earthquakes, and diseases. That is the beginning. There will be crime and people will stop loving one another. It won't be an easy time. Many people will claim to be Me. And they will fool lots of people. They may do things that look like miracles. But don't be tricked. They may tell you that I am in the desert or even in the next room. Don't believe them. I will be coming back, on the clouds, from the East. The gospel must first be taught to all of the nations. Then, the end will come. Immediately after the hard times the sun and the moon will go dark. Even the stars will fall. Then My sign will appear in heaven and I will return on the clouds. A loud trumpet will sound and I will send My angels to the corners of the earth to gather together my people." [2]

When Jesus returns to gather together His people, they will meet Him up in the clouds. There may be two girls shopping together at the mall, then one will be taken up with Jesus, while the other stands there holding her new shoes, wondering how Susie just floated up into the sky like that. Imagine a couple of baseball teams playing. The score is tied, seven to seven. Suddenly, the pitcher, the third baseman, and a couple of kids sitting on the bench start floating up to meet Jesus in the sky. Game over. For the people who get to meet Jesus in the sky, it is paradise eternally from that moment on. [3] The ones left behind face God's wrath. Yikes!

So, how do you get to be one of those floating into paradise? Jesus warns that many are called, but few are chosen. [4] That means that even though everyone has the opportunity to be saved, to go floating off into the wild blue yonder when Jesus comes back, few will choose to do what it takes. It takes faith. In order to be saved, you must believe in Jesus, [5] believe that He died for your sins, and confess His name. [6] The Bible tells us to repent [7] (turn away from and reject) of our sins and be baptized too. [8] Think of eternal life as a gift to you from Jesus. That is what it is. Someone could give you a birthday present, but you could refuse it. Worse yet, you could not even to bother to show up for your own party. Or you could show up... but too late, after all the guests have gone away.

When Jesus returns, the first thing He is going to do is gather together His people. Only God knows when that will be. Your pastor doesn't know, your mom doesn't know, the preacher on TV doesn't know, the angels don't know, not even Jesus Himself knows. He warns us to be ready. Don't miss the cloud ride to heaven.

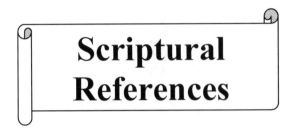

Scriptural References

1 **"But of that day and hour no one knows, not even the angels of heaven, but My Father only. Matthew 24:36**

2 **"But when you hear of wars and rumors of wars, do not be troubled; for such things must happen, but the end is not yet. "For nation will rise against nation, and kingdom against kingdom. And there will be earthquakes in various places, and there will be famines and troubles. These are the beginnings of sorrows. "And the gospel must first be preached to all the nations. "Then if anyone says to you, 'Look, here is the Christ!' or, 'Look, He is there!' do not believe it. "For false christs and false prophets will rise and show signs and wonders to deceive, if possible, even the elect. "But in those days, after that tribulation, the sun will be darkened, and the moon will not give its light; "the stars of heaven will fall, and the powers in the heavens will be shaken. "Then they will see the Son of Man coming in the clouds with great power and glory. "And then He will send His angels, and gather together His elect from the four winds, from the farthest part of earth to the farthest part of heaven. Mark 13:7,8,10,21,22,24-27**

3 **Then we who are alive and remain shall be caught up together with them in the clouds to meet the Lord in the air. And thus we shall always be with the Lord. 1 Thessalonians 4:17**

4 **"For many are called, but few are chosen." Matthew 22:14**

5 **And he brought them out and said, "Sirs, what must I do to be saved?" So they said, "Believe on the Lord Jesus Christ, and you will be saved, you and your household." Acts 16:30,31**

6 **"Therefore whoever confesses Me before men, him I will also confess before My Father who is in heaven. "But whoever denies Me before men, him I will also deny before My Father who is in heaven. Matthew 10:32,33**

7 **and saying, "The time is fulfilled, and the kingdom of God is at hand. Repent, and believe in the gospel." Mark 1:15**

8 'And now why are you waiting? Arise and be baptized, and wash away your sins, calling on the name of the Lord.' Acts 22:16

Discussion Questions

1) How will you know it is Jesus if He comes back in your lifetime?

(<u>You</u> will see Him, clearly, coming on the clouds. Don't worry, you won't miss it if He comes during your lifetime. You'll know it. Don't trust anyone who claims to be Him, unless you saw Him in the clouds yourself.)

2) Will the people who meet Jesus in the clouds all be dead?

(No. Many will never experience death, only eternal life. To the people left behind, they will be missing. Although, as you can imagine, if a bunch of people go floating up to meet Jesus in the clouds, there will likely be witnesses that see it, but stay behind.)

3) No one knows when Jesus will return. It could be today, tomorrow, a hundred or even a thousand years from now. How can you be sure that you are prepared to meet Jesus, if He returned today?

(Make sure that you are saved. If you know Jesus and make Him the Lord of your life, you are prepared.)

"Not everyone who says to Me, 'Lord, Lord,' shall enter the kingdom of heaven, but he who does the will of My Father in heaven. Many will say to Me in that day, 'Lord, Lord, have we not prophesied in Your name, cast out demons in Your name, and done many wonders in Your name?' And then I will declare to them, 'I never knew you; depart from Me, you who practice lawlessness!'" Matthew 7:21-23

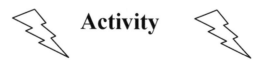

Activity

Directions: Write a short story about the day Jesus returns. You can include how it looks, stories of the people left behind and what they are thinking, etc.

Love

Lesson Twenty-Seven

Scripture of the Week:

"But I say to you, love your enemies, bless those who curse you , do good to those who hate you , and pray for those who spitefully use you and persecute you"

Matthew 5:44

Lesson: Do you know what love is? You would be surprised at how many people don't know the true meaning of love or even how to love. Jesus told us to love our neighbors as ourselves. [1]

It may be easy to love your mom or dad or even your best friend. But, some people aren't very lovable. Some people are mean and nasty and rude. But, Jesus tells us to love our enemies too. [2] Even the rude and nasty and mean people probably love someone they like. So, if you just love people who are nice to you, you aren't doing anything better than they are. But, if you are nice to people who hate you and you give to someone you know is just "using" you, you become more like Jesus. God loved us enough when we were kind of "mean and nasty" ourselves to give us His only Son. [3]

So, how do you past not liking someone to actually love them? The first thing you have to do is separate the person from their sins and their behavior. This isn't easy to do. But, remember that Jesus hung on the cross for that person too. God loved him enough to let His son die for him. Maybe you should try to figure out why. Even some of the most unlovable people usually have good things about them.

Put yourself in their shoes for just a minute. Maybe Mr. "mean and nasty" lives in a real bad situation. His dad ran off before he was born and his mom is always drinking. Maybe he is the only one in the house that takes care of his little brother and sister, making sure they get to eat. Or maybe Mr. "mean and nasty" is always being put down and called "stupid." After a while he starts lashing out at other people. It could be any number of reasons. These aren't excuses. But, maybe Mr. "mean and nasty" has never been shown love by his earthly family, so he doesn't know how to love.

That is where you come in. That is where it becomes your responsibility to show him the love of God. You could do something nice for him. Or, when he says something mean and nasty to you, instead of coming back with something equally mean and nasty, you could try saying something nice instead. You may be surprised at his reaction. Or you may not. He may just continue to be mean and nasty. And if he does, just pray for him. After a while, your smile or kind word may be answered with a smile from Mr. "mean and nasty." Maybe he won't be so "mean and nasty" after all.

When Jesus walked the earth, He hung out with all the "mean and nasties." The church people got real upset about this. They were following Him, why shouldn't he hang out with them? But, Jesus got onto to them. He told them, "If you aren't sick, you don't need to go to the doctor. It is the sinners that need to know Me. You already do." [4] Turns out those mean and nasties Jesus was hanging out with, teaching, turned out to be pretty important believers. Some of them even became His disciples. [5]

Love is a "fruit of the Spirit." [6] In order to get fruit on a tree, you have to take care of it and nurture it. Love is kind of like that. You aren't born with it. Your parents may love you and God definitely loves you. But, in order for you to love back, you have to learn how to love. It is easy if you are surrounded by love. But, if you aren't in a loving environment and don't know how much Jesus loves you, it is harder. There are a lot of people out there like that. The best way to teach them is to show them Christ's love in your actions. If you have Jesus living inside you, you have all you need to do that.

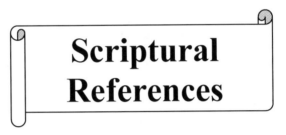

Scriptural References

1   'Honor your father and your mother,' and, 'You shall love your neighbor as yourself.' " Matthew 19:19

2   But I say to you, love your enemies, bless those who curse you, do good to those who hate you, and pray for those who spitefully use you and persecute you" Matthew 5:44

3   But God, who is rich in mercy, because of His great love with which He loved us, even when we were dead in trespasses, made us alive together with Christ (by grace you have been saved), and raised us up together, and made us sit together in the heavenly places in Christ Jesus,   Ephesians 2:4-6

4   Now it happened, as Jesus sat at the table in the house, that behold, many tax collectors and sinners came and sat down with Him and His disciples. And when the Pharisees saw it, they said to His disciples, "Why does your Teacher eat with tax collectors and sinners?" When Jesus heard that, He said to them, "Those who are well have no need of a physician, but those who are sick. But go and learn what this means: 'I desire mercy and not sacrifice.' For I did not come to call the righteous, but sinners, to repentance." Matthew 9:10-13

5   Now the names of the twelve apostles are these: first, Simon, who is called Peter, and Andrew his brother; James the son of Zebedee, and John his brother; Philip and Bartholomew; Thomas and Matthew the tax collector; James the son of Alphaeus, and Lebbaeus, whose surname was Thaddaeus;   Matthew 10:2,3

6 But the fruit of the Spirit is love, joy, peace, longsuffering, kindness, goodness, faithfulness, Galatians 5:22

Discussion Questions

1) What do you do if - no matter how hard you try - you can't seem to love a particular person?

(Try harder. Talk to God about it. Ask Him to show you why you are having a hard time with this one. He may show you that you have some unforgiveness towards this person.)

2) What do you do if you don't really know how to love (or you know someone like this)?

(First, face every problem with prayer. Talk to God and ask Him to help. If you take your eyes off yourself and try serving God, by helping others... you are watering the seed of love that God planted in you before you were born.)

3) What do you do if - no matter how nice you are to someone, they are still mean and nasty to you?

(You pray for them, then don't worry about it anymore.)

"But, I say to you, love your enemies, bless those who curse you, do good to those who hate you, and pray for those who spitefully use you and persecute you.   Matthew 5:44

And whoever will not receive you nor hear your words, when you depart from that house or city, shake of the dust from your feet." Matthew 10:14

Activity

Directions: Break the class into small groups. Have each group make up and act out a skit showing the fruit of the Spirit, Love. (Their page may be used to write down their lines, acting notes, etc.)

115

Joy

Lesson Twenty-Eight

Scripture of the Week:
...this day is holy unto our Lord: neither be you sorry; for the joy of the LORD is your strength.

Nehemiah 8:10

Lesson: Have you ever met anyone that seems happy, no matter what? Even when things in their life appear to be terrible, they manage to smile, laugh, and crack a joke? They have the joy of the Lord in their heart. The joy of the Lord gives you strength to stand against the most terrible circumstances, and be happy anyway. [1] It is something that is deep within, but overflows to the people around.

Maybe you know someone like this. Maybe she just tripped in the hallway at school, books flying everywhere, looking like quite the fool. And you think to yourself, "If that happened to me, I would be crawling into the nearest locker, wanting to die." But, instead of getting all embarrassed, she just sits on the floor, howling with laughter. Or maybe, you know someone who is in a bad situation. Maybe some tragedy just happened to him. But, he is able to make jokes and laugh and carry on, despite the circumstances. These people have discovered the joy of the Lord, and it is alive and well in them.

So what is the "Joy of the Lord?" It is a supernatural dose of God's sense of humor and happiness. If you have it, you have a touch of God's emotions living inside. God has a great sense of humor. Just look around. Think about it... a giraffe? It's a yellow horse with a long neck and spots. Sometimes the joke is on you. Maybe you are spouting off about how silly Johnny looks with his "Jesus Freak" shirt on. But, a couple of years later, you are sporting the latest in "Jesus Freak" attire. Of course, by then, you get a chuckle out of it yourself. We were made in God's image, with many of His emotions. So, of course joy and a sense of humor are going to be part of your makeup.

The neat thing about the joy of the Lord, is it let's you withstand the tough times, without crumbling. It not only makes things bearable, but you can have some fun during those times too. And it chases away dread. You know what dread is. It is that feeling you get when it is bedtime Sunday night and you suddenly realize that you forgot to do your homework. If you are worried about something, the joy of the Lord is there to see you through. It works hand in hand with the peace of God, which destroys worry.

So, how do you get the joy of the Lord? It is a fruit of the Spirit, [2] like love, so it must be grown. Reading the Bible and praying helps. But, the joy of the Lord comes with knowing that Christ is with us and His angels are watching over us. [3] Life is a gift and meant to be enjoyed. [4] You cannot control many of the bad things that happen in life. But, you can control the way you

117

react to them. Remember that being upset about something does nothing to help change a situation. [5] So, you might as well look for all the little joys that God has to offer... and enjoy!

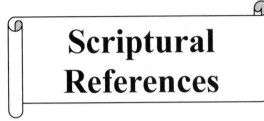

Scriptural References

1   **Then he said to them, "Go your way, eat the fat, drink the sweet, and send portions to those for whom nothing is prepared; for this day is holy to our LORD. Do not sorrow, for the joy of the LORD is your strength." Nehemiah 8:10**

2   **But the fruit of the Spirit is love, joy, peace, longsuffering, kindness, goodness, faithfulness, Galatians 5:22**

3   **"Have I not commanded you? Be strong and of good courage; do not be afraid, nor be dismayed, for the LORD your God is with you wherever you go." Joshua 1:9**

4   **I know that nothing is better for them than to rejoice, and to do good in their lives and also that every man should eat and drink and enjoy the good of all his labor—it is the gift of God. Ecclesiastes 3:12,13**

5   **"Which of you by worrying can add one cubit to his stature? Matthew 6:27**

Discussion Questions

1) If you have the joy of the Lord, are you always happy?
   (No. Even Jesus got angry or sad at times. But, when you have that joy inside you... it will come bubbling back up again.)

 **Activity**

Directions: How many ways can you name to spread the Joy of the Lord?

Peace

Lesson Twenty-Nine

Lesson: Her world is crumbling around her. Her mom and dad are getting divorced. She has to move to a different city, switch schools, and make all new friends. Susie's life is changing drastically. She is about to leave behind every thing she ever knew. But, she is not worried. What? Everything has turned upside down for her, why isn't she worried? Susie has the peace of God. She knows that everything will turn out okay. [1]

Oh, Susie wasn't this calm at first. She cried and yelled and screamed. Of course, none of that did anything to change her circumstances. She had no control over the changes that were about to occur in her life. All she could control was her own reaction. She tried to get her mom to make her feel better about things. But, Susie's mom wasn't much help. She was too busy worrying about finding a new job and moving. Plus, she didn't really want a divorce, so she has been crying a lot lately herself. No, Susie had to find someone else to help her deal with things. Her mom had enough going on already. And Susie didn't want to make her mom feel any worse than she did already. Susie couldn't talk to her Dad either. He was wrapped up in his problems and feeling pretty guilty about the whole divorce thing. He had a hard time facing Susie. Susie's friends didn't know what to tell her, other than they would miss her and they wished she wasn't moving.

So, Susie turned to her Heavenly Father. She started talking to God. No one ever really taught her any special prayers. So, she just started talking to Him like He was her best friend. At first she was mad at Him. She thought it was God's fault for not keeping her mom and dad together. God listened patiently as Susie went on and on. "Why didn't You keep them together?" After a while though, she calmed down. She remembered that God gives everyone freewill. She knew that God wouldn't force people to stay together against their will. Then she cried about having to leave all of her friends behind and how scary it will be to move to a new place and start a new school. But, Susie remembered that God did not give us a spirit of fear. [2] The devil was trying to make her afraid. So, Susie picked up one of her weapons against the devil, her Bible. She started skimming through it. Then, suddenly the words jumped out. It was if God Himself spoke them out loud to her. **"All things work together for good for those that love the Lord."** [3] Susie smiled. She knew God had been listening to her. "God," she said (Susie had learned that she didn't have to say a special prayer for God to listen to her.) "I know that this thing is going to work out. I am just going to give all this worry to you. I don't need it anyway. From now on, I am just going to leave this in Your hands. And if I start to worry about it again, please have the Holy Spirit remind me of this scripture that You just showed me. In Jesus' name, thank You God. Amen."

The worst of it was over for Susie. Things didn't suddenly become real easy. But, she had the peace of God in her now. Every once in a while the devil would try to sneak back in and make her afraid again. But, as soon as Susie realized what was happening, she would just tell that devil to "shut up in the Name of Jesus." Then, she would reread her scripture, which she had written on a little piece of paper and hung up in her new school locker. It made her feel better every time. Susie couldn't keep her parents from getting divorced. But, she learned that she could have the peace of God in her heart by praying, reading her Bible, and leaving things up to God.

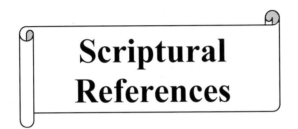

Scriptural References

1 Be anxious for nothing, but in everything by prayer and supplication, with thanksgiving, let your requests be made known to God; and the peace of God, which surpasses all understanding, will guard your hearts and minds through Christ Jesus. Philippians 4:6-7

2 For God has not given us a spirit of fear, but of power and of love and of a sound mind. 2 Timothy 1:7

3 And we know that all things work together for good to those who love God, to those who are the called according to His purpose. Romans 8:28

Discussion Questions

1) What does it mean to "give all of your worry to God" like Susie did?
   (Susie had no control over the things that were about to happen. Worrying didn't help. It just made her feel sick to her stomach. So, every time she would start to worry, she just said to herself, "I'm not going to worry about this. I am going to let God handle it. He's in

charge here." She gave control, and the worry that went with it, to God. Susie never really had control of the situation anyway, she just worried like she did.)

2) One of the hardest things to do is "give your worry to God." How do you do it?
(First, know that God is in charge and your worrying won't help anything. Tell God you trust Him to work things out. Then, find a few scriptures to keep reminding yourself that God has control, like Susie did. Write them down and put them somewhere that you can easily read them, when you need to.)

Activity

Directions: Write down everything that you ever worry about. When you are finished give your worries to God. Put the list in the collection plate or leave it at the altar railing.
(Teacher note: Coordinate with necessary people in the church for this activity.)

Longsuffering
Lesson Thirty

Scripture of the Week:
"By your patience possess your souls.
Luke 21:19

Lesson: Longsuffering? That sure doesn't sound like much fun. I don't think I want any of that fruit...

Think of longsuffering as patience. God is longsuffering towards us. That means He puts up with a lot from us. It is His heart's desire that everyone should share the joy of an eternal life. So, He is patient with mankind. He is hoping as many people as possible will choose "The Way to life," Jesus. [1]

God is patient with us. [2] That means He expects us to be patient with each other. [3]

Think about the last time that you lost patience with someone. Maybe your little brother got into your stuff again. You have told him time and time again not to mess with your stuff. This time he broke something of yours. That was the final straw. You march into his room and break something of his. He starts crying. "I told you it was an accident. I'm sorry. You didn't have to break my favorite toy." He is heartbroken. But, it is all his fault, right? You told him to stay out of your stuff. You have told him a hundred times. Even your mom told him to keep out. He deserved what he got.

Stop. Think a minute. When was the last time you did something you weren't supposed to? Maybe you have a bad habit of saying God's name in vain. You may have just done it again when you saw what your brother broke. But, how many times have you been told not to say God's name in vain? [4] Even if your parents have never told you not to, the Bible is very plain. Your own heart has probably told you it is wrong. How many times have you heard the Ten Commandments? That one is commandment number three. It says "God will not hold him guiltless who takes His name in vain." In other words... it is all your fault for doing it. God told you time and time again not to do it. Do you want to get what you deserve for breaking God's law?

Aren't you glad God is patient with us? Don't you want Him to continue to be? Next time your patience is wearing thin, think about the last time God had to be patient with you. It may have been last week, or yesterday, or even just this morning.

Longsuffering works with forgiveness. If you immediately forgive someone when they do something wrong to you, it is much easier to be patient than when you let offense after offense build up. If you haven't forgiven someone for what they did to you last year, how are you going to have patience left to deal with what they do wrong today?

Longsuffering... patience is a fruit of the Spirit. [5] A good tree bears good fruit. Study the word of God and talk to Him about how to "grow" this good fruit.

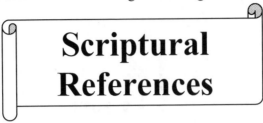

Scriptural References

1   **and consider that the longsuffering of our Lord is salvation—as also our beloved brother Paul, according to the wisdom given to him, has written to you, 2 Peter 3:15**

2   **The Lord is not slack concerning His promise, as some count slackness, but is longsuffering toward us, not willing that any should perish but that all should come to repentance. 2 Peter 3:9**

3   **Therefore, as the elect of God, holy and beloved, put on tender mercies, kindness, humility, meekness, longsuffering; bearing with one another, and forgiving one another, if anyone has a complaint against another; even as Christ forgave you, so you also must do. But above all these things put on love, which is the bond of perfection. Colossians 3:12-14**

4   **"You shall not take the name of the LORD your God in vain, for the LORD will not hold him guiltless who takes His name in vain. Exodus 20:7**

5   **But the fruit of the Spirit is love, joy, peace, longsuffering, kindness, goodness, faithfulness, Galatians 5:22**

Discussion Questions

1) How many times should you forgive someone?
   (Seventy times seven... or in other words... as many times as necessary.)

2) Do you have to forgive someone, even if they don't ask you to?
   (Yes. Your act of forgiveness has more to do with you, than with them.)

3) What happens if you don't forgive someone?

(God will not forgive someone who does not forgive others. Besides, unforgiveness in your life leads to lack of patience, anger, sadness, hurt, and a lot of other stuff you don't want. When you don't forgive someone, it hurts you much more than it hurts them.)

4) Do you have to tell someone "I forgive you" when you forgive them of something.

(It wouldn't hurt. You may gain a friend. But, sometimes that is not always possible. And sometimes that isn't something you should do. For instance, if someone has hurt you... maybe done something really bad to you, but they are still a threat to you... you wouldn't want to go anywhere near them. You can forgive them in your heart. That doesn't mean you have to give them an opportunity to harm you again. Don't worry, God knows your heart.)

Activity

B	F	Y	Q	Y	O	G	U	F	R
F	P	W	A	T	G	I	F	E	N
G	C	E	P	O	D	S	S	D	F
E	S	G	W	G	F	Q	F	W	D
Q	G	F	Y	O	Q	U	F	G	R
W	S	Q	O	U	F	L	S	W	Q

Follow the directions below. You will be left with a message from Luke 21:19. Write the message here. (Answer is scripture of the week.)

"By your patience possess your souls.   Luke 21:19

1) If Jesus saves, cross out all of the Q's.
   If you don't need Jesus to get to heaven, cross out all the S's.

2) If God is impatient with us, cross out all the E's.
   If God is patient with us, cross out all the D's.

3) If it is OK to use God's name in vain, cross out all the P's.
   If it is a sin to use God's name in vain, cross out all the W's.

4) If it is OK not to forgive someone who has sinned against you for the seventh time, cross out all the Y's.

If God expects us to forgive someone seventy times seven times, cross out all the F's.

5) If patience (longsuffering) is a fruit of the Spirit, cross out all the G's.
   If patience (longsuffering) is a fruit of sin, cross out all the A's.

Gentleness and Kindness

Lesson Thirty-One

Scripture of the Week:

"So which of these three do you think was neighbor to him who fell among the thieves?" And he said, "He who showed mercy on him." Then Jesus said to him, "Go and do likewise."

Luke 10:36

Lesson: There is a gentleness of the Spirit that speaks softly to your heart. Jesus was called the Lamb of God, not just because He was given as a sacrifice, like so many baby sheep were given, but because a lamb is a gentle creature. Jesus won hearts by His gentle, loving ways.[1]

The townspeople brought a woman to him who had been caught with a man that wasn't her husband. At the time, the punishment for adultery was stoning to death. The townspeople wanted to stone her. She kneeled at Jesus' feet, ashamed. But, Jesus told the people, "Let him without sin cast the first stone." Suddenly these people who were ready to kill a woman for what she did wrong, were forced to look at themselves and their own wrongdoings. One by one, they dropped their rocks and walked away. Jesus had every right to yell at the woman, to make her feel worse for what she did. But, He didn't. He looked at her and said, "Woman, where are your accusers? Does no one condemn you?" They were all gone. She looked up and saw the stones on the ground. "No one, Lord." "Then neither do I. Go and sin no more." Jesus knew that she was sorry for what she had done. It was not necessary to yell at her. Jesus was gentle with the woman. And you can bet that woman never committed adultery again.[2]

Do you treat the people around you with gentleness? When someone does something bad to you, but asks you for forgiveness, do you make them feel worse? Or do you gently forgive and forget? If you see someone trip over their own feet and fall flat on their face, embarrassing themselves, do you howl with laughter at them? Or do you let the gentleness of God take over and offer a hand to help them up?

Can you think of someone that you know that has the gentleness of God? You like to be around them, don't you? People with the gentleness of God draw people to them.

People with the kindness of God are like that too. They do things for other people just because they want to help them. Maybe it is something as simple as holding a door open for a lady pushing a baby stroller or something as tough as giving someone CPR. Whatever it is, it is usually done automatically, without thinking. They don't do it because they want to be a hero or they want other people to do stuff for them. They do it out of love... love for other people and love for the Lord.

Jesus said, "When I was hungry, you gave Me food. When I was thirsty, you gave Me a drink. And when I was naked, you clothed Me." But the people wanted to know, "When were

You hungry? When were you thirsty? When did we do these things?" Jesus answered, "When you did these things for My people, you did it for Me." [3]

When you are gentle and kind to God's people, it is the same as being gentle and kind to Jesus. But, when you are rude and mean to God's people, it is the same as being rude and mean to Jesus. Kind and gentle people are loved on this earth. People like to be around them. But, those with the gentleness and kindness of the Spirit do it out of love for the Lord. Their real reward is in heaven. Little acts of kindness may go unnoticed on earth, but in heaven, they are cheered!

Scriptural References

1 **You have also given me the shield of Your salvation; Your right hand has held me up, Your gentleness has made me great. Psalm 18:35**

2 **Then the scribes and Pharisees brought to Him a woman caught in adultery. And when they had set her in the midst, they said to Him, "Teacher, this woman was caught in adultery, in the very act. "Now Moses, in the law, commanded us that such should be stoned. But what do You say?" This they said, testing Him, that they might have something of which to accuse Him. But Jesus stooped down and wrote on the ground with His finger, as though He did not hear. So when they continued asking Him, He raised Himself up and said to them, "He who is without sin among you, let him throw a stone at her first." And again He stooped down and wrote on the ground. Then those who heard it, being convicted by their conscience, went out one by one, beginning with the oldest even to the last. And Jesus was left alone, and the woman standing in the midst. When Jesus had raised Himself up and saw no one but the woman, He said to her, "Woman, where are those accusers of yours? Has no one condemned you?" She said, "No one, Lord." And Jesus said to her, "Neither do I condemn you; go and sin no more." John 8:3-11**

3 **'for I was hungry and you gave Me food; I was thirsty and you gave Me drink; I was a stranger and you took Me in; 'I was naked and you clothed Me; I was sick and you visited Me; I was in prison and you came to Me.' "Then the righteous will answer Him, saying, 'Lord, when did we see You hungry and feed You, or thirsty and give You drink? 'When did we see You a stranger and take You in, or naked and clothe You? 'Or when did we see You sick, or in prison, and come to You?' "And the King will answer and say to them, 'Assuredly, I say to you, inasmuch as you did it to one of the least of these My brethren, you did it to Me.' Matthew 25:35-40**

Discussion Questions

1) How do the fruits of the Spirit, gentleness and kindness help the Kingdom of God?

(If you are a representative of the Kingdom and you are gentle and kind, it makes people want to be a part of the Kingdom too.)

2) Who do you find it hardest to be kind and gentle to?

(People who aren't nice to you? Your family?)

3) What can you do to remind yourself to be kind and gentle?

(Try studying the parts of the Bible that shows Jesus being kind and gentle. Think of times that Jesus, or other people have been kind and gentle to you, even though you may not have deserved it. Post a scripture or two about being kind and gentle someplace that you will see it often - especially in the place you may forget the most often ... i.e. in your school locker or on your refrigerator)

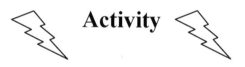 **Activity**

Directions: Jesus told a story about the gentleness and kindness shown by a Good Samaritan. Act out the story. Students may use the bottom of their page to write down lines if they need to.

The Good Samaritan

"A certain man went down from Jerusalem to Jericho, and fell among thieves, who stripped him of his clothing, wounded him, and departed, leaving him half dead. "Now by chance a certain priest came down that road. And when he saw him, he passed by on the other side. "Likewise a Levite, when he arrived at the place, came and looked, and passed by on the other side. "But a certain Samaritan, as he journeyed, came where he was. And when he saw him, he had compassion. "So he went to him and bandaged his wounds, pouring on oil and wine; and he set him on his own animal, brought him to an inn, and took care of him. "On the next day, when he departed, he took out two denarii, gave them to the innkeeper, and said to him, 'Take care of him; and whatever more you spend, when I come again, I will repay you.'" Luke 10: 30-35

Goodness

Lesson Thirty-Two

Scripture of the Week:
Every good gift and every perfect gift is from above, and comes down from the Father of lights, with whom there is no variation of shadow of turning.

James 1:17

Lesson: How many times in your life have you been told to "be good?"... maybe about a million by now? But, what does it mean to be good and what is the difference between you being good and the goodness of God?

Jesus tells us that no one is good except One, that is God. [1] Someone called Jesus good and He corrected him. So, if Jesus did not even consider Himself good, how could we possibly "be good?"

Jesus went on to tell the man, "If you want to enter into life, keep the commandments." [2] In other words, following God's commandments is a good starting place. But, the man's response was that he has always followed God's commandments. "What else should I do?" [3] The man was looking for that one "good thing" that he should do to receive life.

Then, Jesus told him to sell everything he had, give the money to the poor, and follow Him. [4] Does this mean in order to be "good enough" to get to heaven, you have to sell all your stuff and give the money to the poor? No.

First, we must remember that we do not get into heaven by "good things" that we do. We go to heaven because Jesus died for our sins. Accepting Jesus is the only "good" thing that we can do to get into heaven. So, what about selling all of our stuff?

Jesus knew this man. He knew that all his "stuff" was more important to him than God was. [5] Jesus was telling him to get his priorities straight. God first, the rest later. Jesus knew that if the man would put God first, his heart would desire to do good anyway.

Then, what is the goodness of God? The goodness of God is all those wonderful things He has done for us because He loves us... like creating the earth and everything in it, sending His Son to die for our eternal salvation, and blessing us again and again. If you have the goodness of God, from the Holy Spirit, living inside you, you will do good things out of love too. But, the goodness of God is not just about doing good things. It is also about being a good person.

So where does that leave us? If we "act good," following God's commandments, we are halfway there. But, if we put God first in our lives, [6] He will show us His goodness. [7] And He will teach us how to be good people and show goodness to others. Like all of the other fruits of the Spirit, it takes reading God's instruction manual (the Bible) to learn how to "be good." And it takes listening to the Teacher who speaks to our hearts to receive the goodness of the Spirit.

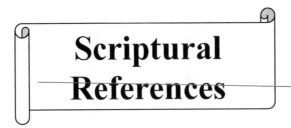

Scriptural References

1 & 2 So He said to him, "Why do you call Me good? No one is good but One, that is, God. But if you want to enter into life, keep the commandments." Matthew 19:17

3 The young man said to Him, "All these things I have kept from my youth. What do I still lack?" Matthew 19:20

4 Jesus said to him, "If you want to be perfect, go, sell what you have and give to the poor, and you will have treasure in heaven; and come, follow Me." Matthew 19:21

5 But when the young man heard that saying, he went away sorrowful, for he had great possessions. Matthew 19:22

6 "You shall have no other gods before Me. Exodus 20:3

7 Oh, how great is Your goodness, Which You have laid up for those who fear You, Which You have prepared for those who trust in You In the presence of the sons of men! Psalm 31:19

Discussion Questions

1) Is having a lot of money bad?

(No. But, loving money and serving it is. Jesus tells us that you can not serve two masters. You can not serve God and serve money at the same time. That doesn't mean that if you are rich, you are bad. But, it does mean that if money is more important to you than God, you have a big problem. Don't spend all of your time and energy chasing a bunch of money. Keep your priorities straight. God always comes first.)

2) If you act really well all the time and you are a good person, will you go to heaven?

(You don't get to heaven by being good. You can be one of the best people on earth, but if you never accept Jesus as your savior, you will not go to heaven. Jesus bought our tickets to heaven when He died on the cross. Your ticket is free. All you have to do is ask Jesus into your heart, ask Him to forgive your sins, and have faith in Him. Then, you get your "ticket to heaven."

3) So, if you can get to heaven by Jesus, instead of by being good, why bother being good?

(If you truly have Jesus living in your heart, your desire will be to do good.)

4) How does the gift of goodness help the Kingdom of God?

(If you are showing people the goodness of God, they will want some of it too. They will want to know where and how to get it. When you show the goodness of God to others, you are "letting your Jesus show." People will want to get to know that Jesus.)

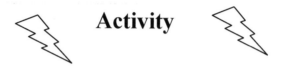

Activity

Directions: Describe a "good" person. You might tell what a "good" person does, how you can tell if someone is good, etc.

Faithfulness

Lesson Thirty-Three

Scripture of the Week:
...the just shall live by his faith.

Habakkuk 2:4

Lesson: Faithfulness is a fruit of the Spirit. It takes having God living in us to truly believe, trust, and be loyal to Him. It sounds funny, doesn't it? We have to God living in us to believe in Him. But, to have true faithfulness we need the Spirit of God to help.

It isn't as strange as it seems. You believe in God. But, maybe sometimes for just a minute you start wondering if there really is a God. Does that mean you really don't believe in God?

You trust God. But, then your parents tell you they are getting divorced. Your life is about to turn upside down. The Bible tells you that "all things work together for the good for those that love the Lord." But, you aren't so sure. Is God really going to work this thing out okay?

You are loyal to God. But, your best friend invites you to a slumber party. And while you are there, they start playing with a Ouiji board. You know it is wrong. It is against God. And you are in the devil's territory. Do you make a stand and tell your friends the truth? If they don't listen, do you call your mom to pick you up? Or do you join right in, so you don't have to be embarrassed by being loyal to God? [1]

Faithfulness is the belief, trust in and loyalty to God. [2] If you are a little lacking in these areas, you are among Bible greats. Peter, one of Jesus' disciples, had a little problem with faithfulness.

Remember the story of Jesus walking on water? He had been teaching all day. As He sent the crowds away He sent His disciples on their way too. Jesus told them to go ahead and take the boat out. He would catch up with them later. They must have really wondered how He was going to do that. A few hours later, Jesus walked out to the boat, stepping over waves. But, when His disciples saw Him walking on the water, they were afraid. They thought He was a ghost. Jesus told them not to worry, it was Him. But, Peter wasn't so sure. He said, "If it is You, Lord, make me come out to You." So, Jesus said, "Come on out!" Then Peter walked on the water. He actually walked on the water, like Jesus. But, when he looked down at the waves, he got scared. He was in deep water and suddenly his trust in Jesus was a little weak. He began to sink. Jesus reached out His hand, grabbed Peter and said, "O you of little faith. Why did you doubt?" [3]

But, that wasn't the only time Peter lacked faithfulness. When the Roman soldiers came for Jesus, Peter denied that he even knew Jesus. Forget loyalty. Three times during that night Peter

137

told people that he didn't even know Jesus. [4] In the end, Peter got it together though. And he ended up with the keys to heaven. [5]

So, how do you receive faithfulness of the Spirit? Just like you receive the rest of the fruit of the Spirit. You study the word of God and you pray.

Next time you feel like the man who wanted his child healed…. Jesus asked him, "Do you believe?" He said with tears in his eyes, "Lord, I believe." He wanted so much to believe. Just do what he did. The next words out of his mouth were, "Help my unbelief!" Jesus healed the man's child. [6]

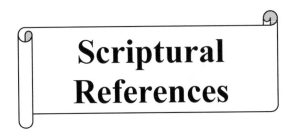

Scriptural References

1 "And blessed is he who is not offended because of Me." Matthew 11:6

2 Oh taste and see that the Lord is good; Blessed is the man who trusts in Him! Psalm 34:8

3 And Peter answered Him and said, "Lord, if it is You, command me to come to You on the water." So He said, "Come." And when Peter had come down out of the boat, he walked on the water to go to Jesus. But when he saw that the wind was boisterous, he was afraid; and beginning to sink he cried out, saying, "Lord, save me!" And immediately Jesus stretched out His hand and caught him, and said to him, "O you of little faith, why did you doubt?" Matthew 14:28-31

4 But he denied it before them all, saying, "I do not know what you are saying." But again he denied with an oath, "I do not know the Man!" Then he began to curse and swear, saying, "I do not know the Man!" Immediately a rooster crowed. Matthew 26:70,72,74

5 "And I also say to you that you are Peter, and on this rock I will build My church, and the gates of Hades shall not prevail against it. "And I will give you the keys of the kingdom of heaven, and whatever you bind on earth will be bound in heaven, and whatever you loose on earth will be loosed in heaven." Matthew 16:18,19

6 Immediately the father of the child cried out and said with tears, "Lord, I believe; help my unbelief!" Mark 9:24

Discussion Questions

1) Why do you think that God gave Peter the keys to heaven even though he lacked faithfulness and he denied that he knew Jesus?

(Peter repented. He was sorry that he denied Jesus and he turned his life around. He preached the word of God and healed many people through the Holy Spirit.)

2) How was Peter able to walk on the water like Jesus?

(His faith allowed him to do miracles. When he lost his faith, he lost the power to do miracles. It was by the power of God that he walked on water. But, the power of God works through people by faith only.)

3) How does having faithfulness of the Spirit help build the kingdom of God?

(God needs people who believe in Him, trust Him, and are loyal to Him to be witnesses on this earth in order to help build the kingdom of God.)

4) How do you react when you are in "deep water" like Peter? Do you lose faith?

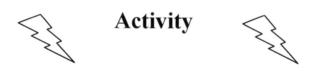

Activity

Directions: Draw a picture of when Peter loses His faith in Jesus. Then draw a picture of what would have happened if Peter had not lost his faith.

Self Control

Lesson Thirty-Four

Scripture of the Week:
For where your treasure is, there your heart will be also.

Luke 12:34

Lesson: It is probably not hard to imagine that sometimes we all need God's help with self-control. Sometimes we need His help several times a day for this. How nice it would be to have the fruit of self-control with us all the time.

If it weren't for temptation, we wouldn't even have to worry about self-control. But since it is out there... lots of it, let's take a look at where it is coming from and what it looks like.

Temptation to sin comes from the devil. God will never tempt anyone to sin. [1] The devil always will. The devil may use anything or anyone he can to tempt you to sin.

Temptation from the devil is carefully made for you. He knows it does him no good to try to tempt you with something you don't care about. The Lord has angels all around to protect you [2] and to do His work. The devil also has "helpers," which are usually called demons. [3] They don't know your thoughts, but they can watch you and listen to you. This is how they learn about you and what is important to you. They use this knowledge to design temptations to sin just for you.

If it is really important to you to be popular at school, the devil will find a way to use that. Maybe he will convince you through the words of other people that you can be popular by joining a gang. Next thing you know, you could be dishonoring your parents, stealing, or even killing yourself with drugs. Self-control could prevent this.

Maybe your weakness is playing on the computer. At first you just surf the Internet a little bit. But, you get bored surfing the kid stuff and start exploring "adult sites." You peek into the "atheist chat room," just to see what those people are like, or you cruise the New Age belief section. Next thing you know, you are spending more and more time online with unbelievers, allowing yourself to be deceived. Self-control would prevent this too.

There are lots of other temptations... as many different temptations as there are people. The devil even tried to tempt Jesus, three times! [4] Of course, Jesus was filled with the Holy Spirit and He had the fruit of self-control. So, the devil was wasting his time.

Praying and studying the Bible are your best defenses against temptation. Learn to recognize the tricks of the devil. When you aren't sure if something is from the devil, check out your Bible.

And remember this, anything, ANYTHING, that you put above God in your life is a temptation to sin. God comes first, period, end. That means school, sports, family, even church. Jesus said that if anyone loves someone (or something) more than they love Him, they are not worthy of Him.[5]

Make the devil waste his time. Put God first.

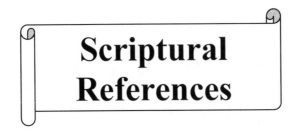

Scriptural References

1   Let no one say when he is tempted, "I am tempted by God"; for God cannot be tempted by evil, nor does He Himself tempt anyone.   James 1:13

2   For He shall give His angels charge over you, To keep you in all your ways.   Psalm 91:11

3   So the great dragon was cast out, that serpent of old, called the devil and satan, who deceives the whole world; he was cast to the earth, and his angels were cast out with him.   Revelation 12:9

4   Then Jesus was led up by the Spirit into the wilderness to be tempted by the devil. Matthew 4:1

5   "He who loves father or mother more than Me is not worthy of Me. And he who loves son or daughter more than Me is not worthy of Me.   Matthew 10:37

Discussion Questions

1) People who lack self-control often end up with addictions to alcohol, drugs, computer games, whatever. How do you know when something becomes an addiction?
   (When something, let's use computer games as an example, becomes more important to you than anything else. You would rather play computer games than talk to your

family, spend time with your friends, eat, sleep. When you are finally doing something other than playing the computer games, if all you can do is think about and talk about them, you know you have a problem. If your friends and family are getting pretty tired of listening to you about the latest computer game... it is time to take a good long look at yourself. You need a priority adjustment.)

2) How and why do addictions happen?

(We were all created to worship and fellowship with God. If you do not have a relationship with Him, you have a gaping hole in your life where that relationship should be. People try to fill that hole with all sorts of things... drugs, computer games, relationships with other people, whatever. That may seem to work, for a while. But, then the person is still unfulfilled. So, they want more drugs, computer games, relationships with other people, whatever. They have an addiction. But, the sad thing is, they are still not fulfilled. The missing puzzle piece is still missing. And only God fits.)

3) What can you do if someone you know has an addiction?

(You can tell them that you think they have a problem, that you love them and that you want to help them. You can pray for them. You can tell them that Jesus is their missing piece. And you can rebuke (In the Name of Jesus) any spirits that are attacking them. But, ultimately, it is their problem. It is their choice. It is their life.)

4) What do you do if it is your addiction?

(Go to God. Tell Him that you have a problem and you want His help. Read your Bible. Talk to your parents, or your pastor, or a trusted adult. Rebuke the devil in the Name of Jesus when you feel Him tempting you. Make God the substitute for your addiction. Whenever you feel the urge to drink, smoke, or play that addicting thing, pick up your Bible instead. Or put on praise music and dance around your room. Or head for some Christian friends. Or start talking to God about it. God promises, **"No weapon formed against you shall prosper." Isaiah 54:17.** That includes weapons of your own making.)

Activity

Directions: List as many things as you can think of that make you lose self control... things that tempt you. Now write down the ways you <u>should</u> deal with these things and how you <u>actually</u> deal with them.

What are the Gifts?

Lesson Thirty-Five

Scripture of the Week:
But the manifestation of the Spirit is given to each one for the profit of all.
1 Corinthians 12:7

Lesson: You have learned about the fruits of the Spirit. They have to be nurtured and grown. But, what about the gifts? In the next few lessons you will learn about the different gifts. But, first, you need to know why God gives them in the first place.

The gifts of the Spirit are given by God to serve His church. He doesn't give them to everyone to just use for themselves. The gifts are meant to be shared. [1] They are used to encourage, to heal, and to bring people to God. Whatever God wants done, He can do through His people by the gifts of the Holy Spirit. All of the gifts come from the same Spirit. [2] Whether you see healing, faith, or miracles in action, it is the Holy Spirit's work you are witnessing.

So how do you get the gifts of the Holy Spirit? God decides who gets what. But, He also tells us we should desire the best gifts. [3] God tells us we should especially want the gift of prophecy, because it encourages, delights, and comforts people.

The way to get the gifts is simply to ask God for them. But, make sure you want the gifts for the right reasons. [4] God will. He knows why you really want them.

Someone can have a gift of the Spirit, without having fruit of the Spirit. But, they don't have God's best. In other words, God may be using Kevin to heal people, but if Kevin is lacking self-control, he won't be able to do all that God has planned for him. In fact, God warns that having a gift, without having love in your heart, makes you nothing. [5]

So, how do you know when you have a gift? Keep praying. Some gifts are obvious, such as tongues. Others take trying them out. If you have asked, and you have faith that you have received a gift, but you don't know which one, keep praying. God will let you know. Often times God gives someone a gift for a specific need. Once that need is taken care of the gift doesn't "show itself" again until it is needed.

So, now you have a gift. Now what? First, know that sometimes you will make mistakes. Maybe you are certain that God has given you a word of knowledge about someone, but it turns out, you are WAY OFF. Maybe it was really a prophecy (something that will happen in the future.) Or maybe you were just dead wrong. It happens. It's God's way of keeping us humble and reminding us to count on Him, not ourselves.

145

Another thing, you need to learn is how to use the gifts with wisdom. Don't shout out something in the middle of the church service that God meant for you to tell someone privately. [6] If you believe you are hearing from God, think about it a minute. Make sure it is the time and the place to pass it on. Maybe God doesn't want you to pass it on. Maybe He just wants you to pray for that person. If you aren't sure, just keep on talking to God about it until you are sure.

Finally, the gifts are meant to encourage God's people. [7] That means you have them to help others. If what you are about to say to someone will make them feel bad about them self, consider that it may not really be from God after all.

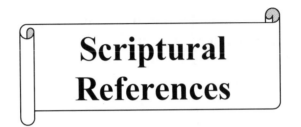

Scriptural References

1   But the manifestation of the Spirit is given to each one for the profit of all.   1 Corinthians 12:7

2   But one and the same Spirit works all these things, distributing to each one individually as He wills.   1 Corinthians 12:11

3   But earnestly desire the best gifts. And yet I show you a more excellent way.   1 Corinthians 12:31

4   Even so you, since you are zealous for spiritual gifts, let it be for the edification of the church that you seek to excel.   1 Corinthians 14:12

5   And though I have the gift of prophecy, and understand all mysteries and all knowledge, and though I have all faith, so that I could remove mountains, but have not love, I am nothing.   1 Corinthians 13:2

6   For God is not the author of confusion but of peace, as in all the churches of the saints.   1 Corinthians 14:33

7   For you can all prophesy one by one that all may learn and all may be encouraged.   1 Corinthians 14:31

Discussion Questions

1) The world, even many churches, say the gifts of the Holy Spirit are dead... that they were only for Jesus' disciples and the ones they baptized. Are they dead?

(Absolutely not. **Jesus is the same yesterday, today, and tomorrow. Hebrews 13:8. And the Holy Spirit will be with us forever. (John 14:16)** He is not here just to hang out with us. He is here for a purpose... and you can be sure He brought His power with Him. Besides, not everyone who received the baptism of the Holy Spirit were Jesus' twelve disciples and those they baptized. John the Baptist was filled with the Holy Spirit from his mother's womb. (Luke 1:15) And he was born before Jesus. But, Jesus warns that **"the world cannot receive (or believe in) the Holy Spirit because it doesn't see Him or know Him. But, you know Him, because He dwells with you and will be in you." (John 14:17)** So, is it any wonder there are so many that do not believe?)

2) Can you use the gifts of the Holy Spirit for yourself?

(Sometimes. Even though they are mainly for others, there are times you can use them for yourself. Since you are part of God's church, He wants you to be encouraged too.)

3) Can you use the gifts of the Holy Spirit for people who don't belong to your church?

(Absolutely. One of the reasons for the gifts is to bring people into the Kingdom of God. But, don't get too worried if you help lead someone to God, and they end up going to a different church. God may have a different place for them in mind. Bless them and send them off with a smile.)

4) Would you like to have a gift or gifts of the Holy Spirit?

Activity

Directions: Unscramble the words to find the gifts of the Holy Spirit.

stoptreetrainin = interpretations
gotuens = tongues
mcarlies = miracles
glashein = healings
gednicrisn fo tirssip = discerning of spirits
doswim = wisdom
gleendkow = knowledge
tihaf = faith
chopprey = prophecy

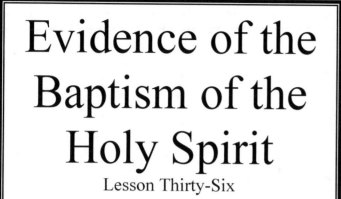

Evidence of the Baptism of the Holy Spirit

Lesson Thirty-Six

Scripture of the Week:

"And these signs will follow those who believe: In My name they will cast out demons; they will speak with new tongues;

Mark 16:17

Lesson: When you receive the baptism of the Holy Spirit, you also receive the ability to pray in tongues. These "tongues" are evidence of the baptism of the Holy Spirit. This prayer language is the language of angels [1] and of God. [2]

When you pray in the Spirit, as it is called, your spirit is speaking directly to the Holy Spirit. You may not know what to pray for, but your spirit knows what you need. And when you pray in the Spirit, the Holy Spirit prays with and for you to God according to God's will. [3] That means, the Holy Spirit knows what you want and need, while at the same time knowing the will of God. So, even if you have no idea of what God wants for you, the Holy Spirit does.

Imagine for a minute you that have a decision to make. Maybe you don't have time to play soccer and violin after school, but you enjoy both. So, you start praying in the Spirit, asking God to lead you in your decision. The Holy Spirit prays on your behalf too. It is called interceding. But, what you don't know is that God intends for you to play with the London Symphony Orchestra one day. But, the Holy Spirit knows the will of God and leads you in the right direction. The choices you make in life may seem random. But, if you allow God, He will lead you in the right direction every time.

Praying in the Spirit encourages you and strengthens you spiritually. [4] And the demons hate it. They usually go running when someone starts praying in the Spirit out loud. They can't stand to hear it. And with those demons running, it becomes easier to concentrate on God. The more you pray the more of God's strength you receive. He works best in your weakness. That is because when you are weak, you are usually more willing to let God take over. He lends you His strength. [5]

When you are baptized with the Holy Spirit, you receive power to do God's work. One of the last things that Jesus told His disciples before He went to heaven was to wait in Jerusalem for the baptism of the Holy Spirit. [6] He said, "These signs will follow those who believe. In My name they will cast out demons. They will speak with new tongues; they will take up serpents; and if they drink anything deadly, it will by no means hurt them. They will lay hands on the sick, and they sick will recover." [7] You will be able to tell others about God without fear. And the Holy Spirit helps you to understand the Bible better. [8] Suddenly, ideas that you never understood before will begin to make perfect sense. The Holy Spirit can do anything He needs through Spirit-filled (those baptized with the Holy Spirit) people. But, you must be willing and open to do God's work.

Remember that the way to be baptized in the Holy Spirit is to want it and to ask God for it.[9] Make the Holy Spirit welcome and learn to follow His voice.[10] And finally, have faith that you have received the baptism of the Holy Spirit.

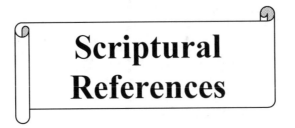

Scriptural References

1   **Though I speak with the tongues of men and of angels, but have not love, I have become sounding brass or a clanging cymbal.   1 Corinthians 13:1**

2   **For he who speaks in a tongue does not speak to men but to God, for no one understands him; however, in the spirit he speaks mysteries.   1 Corinthians 14:2**

3   **Likewise the Spirit also helps in our weaknesses. For we do not know what we should pray for as we ought, but the Spirit Himself makes intercession for us with groanings which cannot be uttered. Now He who searches the hearts knows what the mind of the Spirit is, because He makes intercession for the saints according to the will of God.   Romans 8:26,27**

4   **He who speaks in a tongue edifies himself, but he who prophesies edifies the church. 1 Corinthians 14:4**

5   **And He said to me, "My grace is sufficient for you, for My strength is made perfect in weakness." Therefore most gladly I will rather boast in my infirmities, that the power of Christ may rest upon me. Therefore I take pleasure in infirmities, in reproaches, in needs, in persecutions, in distresses, for Christ's sake. For when I am weak, then I am strong. 2 Corinthians 12:9,10**

6   **"Behold, I send the Promise of My Father upon you; but tarry in the city of Jerusalem until you are endued with power from on high."   Luke 24:49**

7   **"And these signs will follow those who believe: In My name they will cast out demons; they will speak with new tongues; "they will take up serpents; and if they drink anything deadly, it will by no means hurt them; they will lay hands on the sick, and they will recover."   Mark 16:17,18**

8 "But the Helper, the Holy Spirit, whom the Father will send in My name, He will teach you all things, and bring to your remembrance all things that I said to you. John 14:26

9 "If you then, being evil, know how to give good gifts to your children, how much more will your heavenly Father give the Holy Spirit to those who ask Him!"
Luke 11:13

10 "And we are His witnesses to these things, and so also is the Holy Spirit whom God has given to those who obey Him." Acts 5:32

1) What happens is you aren't sure which direction the Spirit is leading you and you choose the wrong way?

(It happens sometimes. You have a decision to make, not between right and wrong. That would be easy. But, between two things that both seem right. You make a decision and it turns out to be the wrong one. Don't worry, God allows U-turns. He can work with you from whatever direction you are facing... turning you around completely, if necessary.)

2) Jesus said that these signs will follow those who believe... **"they will take up serpents; and if they drink anything deadly, it will by no means hurt them"** (Mark 16:17) Does this mean that if you believe in Jesus you can play with snakes and drink poison?

(It wouldn't be a very good idea. God expects you to use wisdom. It wouldn't be very wise to play with snakes or knowingly drink poison. In the time the Bible was written there were not anti-venom shots for snake bites and not all poisons (plants, etc.) were known. So, sometimes, people died from things that could not be helped. God's protection kept His followers from dying from things like this. Of course, now we know which snakes, plants, etc. are poisonous. Even though God's word still rings true, you also are expected to use wisdom not to mess with these things.)

3) What is the difference between the baptism of water and the baptism of fire (Holy Spirit)?

(The baptism of water is for the redemption of sins. That means that you have made a decision to turn away from sinning and live for God. You are asking for and receiving forgiveness of your sins when you are baptized with water. The baptism by fire, which is of the Holy Spirit, is an invitation for God's Spirit to live in and do His work through you.)

4) Why would anyone want the baptism of the Holy Spirit?
   (When you are baptized with the Holy Spirit, you are given power to do God's work. Think of how much more you could do for the Kingdom of God, with His power working in you.)

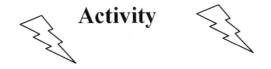

Activity

Directions: Take this time to lay hands on each other and (for those who wish) pray for the baptism of the Holy Spirit. If no one wishes for the baptism of the Holy Spirit, pray for each other anyway. Remember that all you need to do to receive the baptism of the Holy Spirit is to want it, pray for it, and believe that you have received it. No one will force you to speak in tongues. If you want to once you have received the baptism of the Holy Spirit, you have to make the noise, but the Holy Spirit will give you the words. If you have any special prayer requests, write them down here. When it is your turn to be prayed for, you can read this aloud, if you want, to the people praying for you. Or you can just tell your classmates, "I need prayer," without telling them what about. You might want to write down other's prayer requests here, too. That way you can take this home and pray for them later too.

(Teacher **note** : Depending on the "personality" of the class, it may be easier for everyone in the class to pray for one person at once, taking turns going around the room. Or it may be easier to break them into small groups, allowing them to pray for each other within their own group. It may be a little awkward for them at first, but it is usually easier for them to learn to pray with their peers, than in front of the whole church. And if they start now it will be easier for them to pray for others when they are teenagers and into adulthood.)

Tongues / Interpretations

Lesson Thirty-Seven

Scripture of the Week:
(Therefore tongues are for a sign, not to those who believe but to unbelievers); but prophesying is not for unbelievers but for those who believe.

1 Corinthians 14:22

Lesson: The ability to speak in new tongues is evidence of the baptism of the Holy Spirit. [1] But, God doesn't just give that gift to you to prove that you have been baptized in the Holy Spirit. Praying in tongues has real power.

You have learned that demons hate it. But, what can that do for you? Lots. Imagine you are having problems at school. Maybe someone is being really mean to you. Chances are that person is being manipulated by an evil spirit to act that way. Someone doesn't actually have to be possessed to be affected by a demon. (The devil even tried to manipulate Jesus. Of course, it didn't work. But, he tried anyway.) You will learn later how to rebuke evil spirits. In the meantime, though, try praying in tongues.

Remember how the evil spirits fly the other way when you start with the tongues? Whenever someone is mean to you, start praying in tongues. You can do it under your breath, if you want. Don't worry, the demons can hear it loud and clear. But, it isn't your voice they hear. It is the authority of Jesus. He gave His Spirit filled believers the authority He has against satan and his demons. [2] So, what those demons hear is that authority. Try it. See what happens. But, if you aren't a true believer and follower, don't even think about it. Only those who belong to Jesus carry His authority.

The gifts of the Holy Spirit were meant to be used for God's work. So, what else can you do with the gift of tongues? Someone may need you to pray for them. Maybe they have asked you to or maybe you feel they need it. Or maybe the Holy Spirit has prompted you to pray for them. In any case, you don't even know where to begin. What are you supposed to pray for? That is where praying in tongues comes in handy. Not only does the Holy Spirit know God's will for you, He knows it for the whole world. [3]

Just start interceding (remember that means to pray on someone else's behalf). The Holy Spirit will join right in, praying the will of God. After a minute or two of praying in the Spirit, the Holy Spirit may start letting you know what you are praying about. One minute you are praying in tongues for someone, the next minute you start praying for healing in their lungs. You didn't know there was anything wrong with their lungs a minute ago. Maybe they didn't either. But, God led you in that direction. Just follow Him. Then again, you may be praying away, but the Spirit never clues you in to just what you are praying for. That's okay too. Sometimes it is just between that person and God.

So, when you start speaking in tongues will people think you are strange? Probably. It scares some people. The devil has fooled many in the world into believing that speaking in tongues is evil and has come from him. And since the devil has a fake of everything on rare occasion, it could be. But, the Bible tells us over and over that followers of Jesus speak in tongues. It also tells us to think about where we use our prayer language. [4] If an entire church is speaking in tongues and a non-believer walks in, he will think they have all lost their mind. [5] Praying in tongues is a prayer language between you and God. [6] If someone speaks in tongues to the church, it is best to have an interpreter. [7] Even though you may not understand your own prayer language (most people don't), sometimes God gives someone the ability to interpret it. Of course, that is if God wants other people to hear the message. If you are just talking to God, there is no need for an interpreter.

There may be an instance where you feel like praying in tongues with or around an unbeliever. If you feel led to, go ahead. Remember, the gift of tongues is a sign to unbelievers. [8] The Holy Spirit will help the unbeliever handle it. On the other hand, if you feel real uneasy (rather than just a little nervous or self-conscious), it is most likely the Holy Spirit letting you know that person is not quite ready to hear someone speak in tongues yet.

Sometimes the tongues you are speaking in is not a prayer language between you and God. Sometimes it is someone else's language. When the disciples were first filled with the Holy Spirit, they were in Jerusalem, with many people who spoke different languages. Suddenly, the disciples started preaching in all the languages of the people that surrounded them. As you can guess, people were amazed. They knew that the disciples were from Galilee and spoke only their own language. Yet, here they were in Jerusalem, suddenly speaking over fifteen different languages. [9] A few people made fun of them, saying they must be drunk. But, Peter, one of Jesus' disciples stood up and told them, "They are not drunk on wine, like you think they are. It is only nine o'clock in the morning. But, they are filled with the Holy Spirit." [10]

You can be filled with that same Spirit.

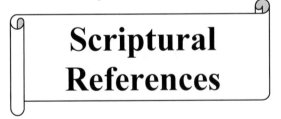

Scriptural References

1   **And they were all filled with the Holy Spirit and began to speak with other tongues, as the Spirit gave them utterance. Acts 2:4**

2   **"Behold, I give you the authority to trample on serpents and scorpions, and over all the power of the enemy, and nothing shall by any means hurt you. Luke 10:19**

3   **Likewise the Spirit also helps in our weaknesses. For we do not know what we should pray for as we ought, but the Spirit Himself makes intercession for us with groanings which cannot be uttered. Now He who searches the hearts knows what the**

mind of the Spirit is, because He makes intercession for the saints according to the will of God.   Romans 8:26,27

4   But if there is no interpreter, let him keep silent in church, and let him speak to himself and to God. 1 Corinthians 14:28

5   Therefore if the whole church comes together in one place, and all speak with tongues, and there come in those who are uninformed or unbelievers, will they not say that you are out of your mind?   1 Corinthians 14:23

6   For he who speaks in a tongue does not speak to men but to God, for no one understands him; however, in the spirit he speaks mysteries.   1 Corinthians 14:2

7   If anyone speaks in a tongue, let there be two or at the most three, each in turn, and let one interpret.   1 Corinthians 14:27

8   Therefore tongues are for a sign, not to those who believe but to unbelievers; but prophesying is not for unbelievers but for those who believe. 1 Corinthians 14:22

9   And they were all filled with the Holy Spirit and began to speak with other tongues, as the Spirit gave them utterance. And there were dwelling in Jerusalem Jews, devout men, from every nation under heaven. And when this sound occurred, the multitude came together, and were confused, because everyone heard them speak in his own language. Then they were all amazed and marveled, saying to one another, "Look, are not all these who speak Galileans? "And how is it that we hear, each in our own language in which we were born? Acts 2:4-8

10 Others mocking said, "They are full of new wine." But Peter, standing up with the eleven, raised his voice and said to them, "Men of Judea and all who dwell in Jerusalem, let this be known to you, and heed my words. "For these are not drunk, as you suppose, since it is only the third hour of the day. "But this is what was spoken by the prophet Joel: 'And it shall come to pass in the last days, says God, That I will pour out of My Spirit on all flesh; Your sons and your daughters shall prophesy, Your young men shall see visions, Your old men shall dream dreams. Acts 2:13-17

Discussion Questions

1) If someone is being mean to you and you start praying in tongues under your breath, will they always stop being mean?

(No. Not all bad behavior is caused by evil spirits. Some people just choose to act that way. But, it wouldn't hurt to try. And if that doesn't stop to them... maybe you should pray in tongues out loud. Imagine their surprise!)

2) Why would anyone want to speak in tongues?

(There is great power in the Holy Spirit. God doesn't give us things for no reason. Jesus told us that His followers would speak in other tongues. Remember that God does everything for a reason.)

3) How does praying in tongues help the kingdom of God?

(There may be many times that you don't know the will of God. Sometimes He will reveal it to you, sometimes He won't. But, when you are praying in tongues, you are praying together with the Holy Spirit and you are praying for God's will to be done.)

Activity

Directions: Find the words hidden in the puzzle. When you find a word, mark through it (instead of circling it). Once you have found all of the words, try to figure out the message that remains. Use the space to write the message. (Teacher note: The remaining message is in bold italics, for your information.)

A	*T*	*H*	*R*	*E*	E	*F*	*O*	*R*	*E*	S	M
N	G	O	D	*T*	*O*	*N*	*G*	*U*	*E*	G	I
G	*S*	J	*A*	*R*	*E*	Y	L	O	H	N	R
E	H	E	*F*	*O*	*R*	*A*	W	*S*	I	I	A
L	E	S	*G*	N	N	O	I	*T*	T	L	C
S	A	U	*O*	T	H	O	S	*S*	E	A	L
W	V	S	*H*	*O*	*B*	E	D	*L*	*I*	E	E
E	E	*V*	*E*	*B*	*U*	T	O	*T*	*O*	H	S
U	N	*N*	*B*	*E*	*L*	*I*	M	*E*	*V*	*E*	*R*

Prophecy
Lesson Thirty-Eight

Scripture of the Week:
For false christs and false prophets will rise and show signs and wonders to deceive, if possible, even the elect.

Mark 13:22

Lesson: The gift of prophecy may be one of the most imitated gifts of God in the world today. For many wonders that God has, the devil has a counterfeit, a fake.

A prophecy is a message received from God, usually through a Spirit-filled Christian, about the future. [1] The Bible is full of prophecies. Many have already come true. Many of them are still in the future. God gives prophecies to people today, mainly to excite, encourage and comfort them. [2] If someone gives you a prophecy, it may be for tomorrow or it may be for twenty years from now. They may be long drawn out speeches, or they may be just a few words. But, one thing they never are... they are never from a psychic.

The psychic hot-line craze is the devil's imitation of God's prophets. The devil has people so busy calling these supposed psychics, they don't even bother to go to God. Ha ha. Just as the devil planned. And look, not only is he keeping them from going to God, he is getting to fill their heads full of lies too. When these fortunes don't come true, people get mad at God... wondering why He doesn't make these great things happen for them. People mad at God don't praise Him. So the devil gets to keep attacking them without fear. And as a bonus, he gets to take all their money too. But, you can't buy a gift of God with money. [3] Most of the people working on the other end of those hot lines are trained to ask lots of questions, and listen closely. Sometimes they get something right by coincidence. More often than not though, their "advice" is so general, you can make it fit just about any situation, if you try hard enough.

There is also something called a spirit of divination. That spirit appears to get things right, mainly because they are communicating with satan's other spies. They may know just enough about your life to make you think they could know the future too.

A slave woman with this spirit of divination kept following Paul (one of Jesus' disciples) all over Macedonia as he was spreading the gospel there. She would shout out things like "These men are the servants of the Most High God, who proclaim to us the way of salvation!" Well, after a few days of having this woman on his heels shouting all the time, Paul got annoyed with it. He finally turned around and said, "I command you in the name of Jesus Christ to come out of her!" And the spirit was cast out of her right then. Her owners were pretty upset with Paul, because they had been making a lot of money off of her "fortune telling." [4] She knew just enough to make people believe she knew it all.

159

You may run into to this spirit one day. But, do you really want to follow the advice of an evil spirit... one of satan's demons whose goal is to destroy you? Wouldn't you rather hear from one of God's prophets? They won't charge you $3.99 a minute.

Of course, there are the old standby imitators of witches, tarot card readers, palm readers, astrologers, people who contact the dead, spiritists (like today's New Age "religion"), etc. God warns that all of these are an abomination to Him. [5] An abomination to God means it is something that God despises. People who practice witchcraft will not inherit the Kingdom of God. You should go to God instead. [6]

A prophet of God is there to give you God's message. God may not have a message He wants to tell you through a prophet right then. A prophet of God won't just make something up so he has something to tell you. He will just tell you that God hasn't given him anything to share with you. Can you imagine the psychic hot line telling you, "Well, we don't really have anything to tell you today. We are going to refund the $5.00 for the first minute we were going to charge you." Yeah, right.

The real gift of prophecy is one of the best gifts of the Spirit to have. God chooses His prophets carefully. But, He tells us to keep wanting it and keep asking for it. [7]

How will you know if you have the gift of prophecy? You can usually tell by looking back. Maybe you have made some pretty outrageous statements to your friends or family. You didn't really think of it at the time. You just sort of blurted out what you thought would happen. It may have sounded really strange, even impossible at the time. But, now you look back, and find that you have been right more times than you have been wrong.

That doesn't mean you should start walking around telling everyone that you are a prophet and handing out prophecies. Prophets are usually in training by God for years. But, small children have been known to give prophecies. It may be that God only needs you to pass along a prophecy once or twice in your lifetime. Or He may have in mind for you to be prophesying on a daily basis. Keep praying and God will let you know what He has in mind for you when the time is right.

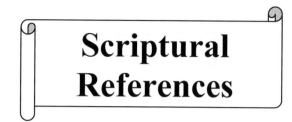

Scriptural References

1. knowing this first, that no prophecy of Scripture is of any private interpretation, for prophecy never came by the will of man, but holy men of God spoke as they were moved by the Holy Spirit. 2 Peter 1:20,21

2. But he who prophesies speaks edification and exhortation and comfort to men. 1 Corinthians 14:3

3. But Peter said to him, "Your money perish with you, because you thought that the gift of God could be purchased with money! Acts 8:20

4. Now it happened, as we went to prayer, that a certain slave girl possessed with a spirit of divination met us, who brought her masters much profit by fortune-telling. This girl followed Paul and us, and cried out, saying, "These men are the servants of the Most High God, who proclaim to us the way of salvation." And this she did for many days. But Paul, greatly annoyed, turned and said to the spirit, "I command you in the name of Jesus Christ to come out of her." And he came out that very hour. But when her masters saw that their hope of profit was gone, they seized Paul and Silas and dragged them into the marketplace to the authorities. And they brought them to the magistrates, and said, "These men, being Jews, exceedingly trouble our city; Acts 16:16-20

5. "There shall not be found among you anyone who makes his son or his daughter pass through the fire, or one who practices witchcraft, or a soothsayer, or one who interprets omens, or a sorcerer, or one who conjures spells, or a medium, or a spiritist, or one who calls up the dead. For all who do these things are an abomination to the LORD, and because of these abominations the LORD your God drives them out from before you. Deuteronomy 18:10-12

6. And when they say to you, "Seek those who are mediums and wizards, who whisper and mutter," should not a people seek their God? Should they seek the dead on behalf of the living? Isaiah 8:19

7. Pursue love, and desire spiritual gifts, but especially that you may prophesy. 1 Corinthians 14:1

Discussion Questions

1) Is a real prophet always right?

(Real prophecies are always right. However, since prophets are human, they will make mistakes sometimes. Like everyone, they may think they are hearing from God, but they aren't. But, God's prophets know that all prophecies must line up with the word of God. So, they will not give prophecies that disagree with the Bible. If they do, they are not speaking on behalf of God.)

2) When you get a prophecy, when will it "come true?"

(God may or may not tell us exactly when the prophecy will come to pass. It could be hours away, days away, or even many years away. If you receive a prophecy, write it down in a special place. Every once in a while, read through it. You may read it one day and recognize that it is coming true that very day.)

3) "But, my friend called a psychic and what he said came true!" Does that mean that they are right sometimes?

(Don't believe them, ever. You can't buy a gift of God with money (Acts 8:20). So, anything coming out of a psychic's mouth is not from God. The world is full of false prophets. They are deceivers of the devil. Next time you see one of those 1-900-psychic ads, check out the small print at the bottom of the screen. It says, "For entertainment use only." That is so they can't be sued for telling lies to people.)

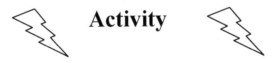

Activity

Directions: Tell a story about someone who pretended they had the gift of prophecy, but really didn't. What harm could someone like that cause? Who might believe in them? How were they "found out" as a fake?

Faith

Lesson Thirty-Nine

Scripture of the Week:
So the Lord said, "If you have faith as a mustard seed, you can say to this mulberry tree, 'Be pulled up by the roots and be planted in the sea,' and it would obey you.

Luke 17:6

Lesson: The gift of faith allows you to believe God for the impossible, despite what things look like. So, how is this different than regular faith? Sometimes things look so bad that we really can't imagine how even God can help. That is when we need a little extra help from God in the faith department. This is especially helpful when you are praying for someone else and their faith is weak. Sometimes you need enough faith for both of you.

Maybe you have heard stories about people who have been in a terrible accident. The doctors tell the family that their loved one will stay in a coma and never recover. Even if they did wake up, they wouldn't be the same person, unable to talk or even think. But, the family prays and believes anyway. Even though it is "medically" impossible, the loved one wakes up and is just fine. With God all things are possible. [1]

There was an old couple who had never been able to have any children. Sarah was ninety. Her husband, Abraham, was ninety-nine. Abraham served the Lord and had great faith. One day, God decided to reward Abraham for his faithfulness by giving him a son. The Lord visited Abraham in his tent to give him the good news. Sarah overheard Him and laughed to herself. "Impossible!" she thought. "I am ninety years old." But, the Lord knew she was laughing in her heart, and said to Abraham, "Why did Sarah laugh? Is anything too hard for the Lord?" Sarah was scared then, and said, "I didn't laugh." [2] She lacked faith. But, Abraham had enough faith for both of them. Despite what seemed absolutely impossible, about a year later, baby Isaac was born to them. [3]

In your life, there may be times when things really do look absolutely impossible... about as impossible as a ninety year old woman having a baby. And even though you have faith in God, you may need a little help. That is what the gift of the Holy Spirit called faith is for.

Maybe your best friend has just come to you and told you that her mom has cancer. The doctors have told her that they can't do anything about it and she only has a year or two to live. But, your next door neighbor just died from the same kind of cancer after five months. What are you going to tell your best friend? She doesn't need to hear about your neighbor. She needs to hear about your God. Pray with her. Pray for her. She may be staring the illness in the face, day in and day out, as her mom gets sicker and weaker. Faith may be a little tough for her as she watches this. This is why it becomes so important for you to have enough faith for both of you. Keep praying and believe that God will give you the gift of faith so you can believe for the impossible!

163

The gift of faith is the ability to believe God's promises, even when every bit of common sense inside you screams that it is impossible. **With God, all things are possible.**

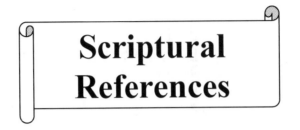

Scriptural References

1   But Jesus looked at them and said to them, "With men this is impossible, but with God all things are possible."   Matthew 19:26

2   And He said, "I will certainly return to you according to the time of life, and behold, Sarah your wife shall have a son." (Sarah was listening in the tent door, which was behind him.) Now Abraham and Sarah were old, well advanced in age; and Sarah had passed the age of childbearing. Therefore Sarah laughed within herself, saying, "After I have grown old, shall I have pleasure, my lord being old also?" And the LORD said to Abraham, "Why did Sarah laugh, saying, 'Shall I surely bear a child, since I am old?' Is anything too hard for the LORD? At the appointed time I will return to you, according to the time of life, and Sarah shall have a son." But Sarah denied it, saying, "I did not laugh," for she was afraid. And He said, "No, but you did laugh!"   Genesis 18:10-15

3   For Sarah conceived and bore Abraham a son in his old age, at the set time of which God had spoken to him. And Abraham called the name of his son who was born to him—whom Sarah bore to him—Isaac.   Genesis 21:2,3

Discussion
Questions

1) If you are having a hard time with your faith, what should you do?

(Dive right into your Bible. **Faith comes by hearing, and hearing by the Word of God. Romans 10:17.** That means that the more of the Word of God you hear, the stronger your faith will be.)

2) How much faith is enough faith?

(So the Lord said, "If you have faith as a mustard seed, you can say to this mulberry tree, 'Be pulled up by the roots and be planted in the sea,' and it would obey you." Luke 17:6) A mustard seed is a tiny seed that grows into a very large plant. So, even a small amount of faith can grow into a tremendous amount.}

3) When Sarah heard that she was going to soon be pregnant, she laughed at the thought of it. But, when she was questioned about her laughing in her heart, she lied and denied it. Sarah obviously lacked faith. So, why did she have a baby a year later?

(God was honoring Abraham's faith. There may be times that you pray for someone that lacks faith. God will honor your faith, too.)

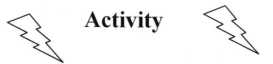

Activity

Directions: What is your biggest dream? Your heart's desire? Is it to be a doctor? To get a little sister? To fly to the moon? Whatever it is, it will take faith to let God show you the way to your heart's desire. Write down whatever it is you want more than anything else in the world. Explain why you want it and how you believe getting it will affect your life. Be sure to put today's date on it!

Take this home and keep it. Talk to God about it. See if you can find a scripture or two that relates to it and write them down here too. Have faith that God's will is going to be done in your life. Pull this out from time to time and pray about it again. When you feel you have received God's answer about it, write down the answer on this page too. Answered prayers help build your faith.

Healing
Lesson Forty

Scripture of the Week:
But He was wounded for our transgressions, He was bruised for our iniquities; The chastisement for our peace was upon Him, And by His stripes we are healed.

Isaiah 53:5

Lesson: Everyone knows that Jesus healed people. He made blind people see, crippled people walk, and dead people live again. But, did you know that Jesus is still healing people today?

When Jesus was beaten and crucified, He bore our sins and our sicknesses. [1] **By His stripes we are healed**. [2] That means that Jesus received "stripes" (the cuts in the skin that are caused by being struck with a whip) so that we did not have to have diseases. But, people do have diseases, does that mean it didn't work?

No. It works very well. There is sin in the world. And with sin comes all the bad stuff, like diseases. But, the good news is, Jesus already bought our healing with His stripes. "By His stripes we are healed" is a promise from God. Not a "maybe" from God. And just like every other gift, you have to have faith to open that gift.

Yes, Jesus is still healing people today. He uses the Holy Spirit working through His people to deliver that healing. His healers usually "lay hands" (place their hands on them) on the sick, while praying for them. [3] They may pray in tongues, or in their own language. They may do both. They may not know what exactly is wrong with the person they are praying for, or they may. Each person is different and God has His healer do exactly what that person needs. The sick person may instantly get better or it may take a little time. And the sick person has to have faith too. [4]

If Johnny has a stomachache and Susie prays for Him. But, Johnny doesn't believe that God can or will heal him. Guess what? Johnny probably isn't going to feel much better. But, if Johnny "receives" healing by believing that Jesus has healed him through Susie's prayers, you can be sure Johnny will be feeling much better soon. Even if his pain doesn't go away the exact second that Susie finishes her prayer, the healing has "been released." That means that Jesus has given Johnny his healing and Johnny's body is getting better. Sometimes, though, healing happens instantly.

Little Tina wore very thick glasses to see. But, one day a man with the gift of healing visited her church. She went up to the front and told him that she didn't want to wear glasses anymore. So, he put his hands on her and prayed for healing. She believed in Jesus completely. And that very instant, her eyes were made perfect. Her mom took her to the eye doctor the next day. He told her, "I don't know how this happened, but she doesn't need these glasses anymore. She has perfect vision." Just two days before Tina couldn't even see past three feet away without glasses. And everything was blurry. But, Jesus healed her.

The Lord does the healing. He just uses people to lay hands on the sick and pray for them. Sometimes, it isn't even necessary to lay hands on the sick. Sometimes it only takes the prayer and the faith. It all depends on what God wants to do.

But, there is one thing you can always count on. God never wants you to be sick. His Son was beaten so that you didn't have to put up with sickness. The price of healing has already been paid. It is a gift of God. Open it.

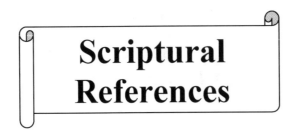

Scriptural References

1   that it might be fulfilled which was spoken by Isaiah the prophet, saying: "He Himself took our infirmities And bore our sicknesses."   Matthew 8:17

2   But He was wounded for our transgressions, He was bruised for our iniquities; The chastisement for our peace was upon Him, And by His stripes we are healed.   Isaiah 53:5

3   "they will take up serpents; and if they drink anything deadly, it will by no means hurt them; they will lay hands on the sick, and they will recover." Mark 16:18

4   But Jesus turned around, and when He saw her He said, "Be of good cheer, daughter; your faith has made you well." And the woman was made well from that hour.   Matthew 9:22

Discussion Questions

1) What happens if someone is very sick, so you pray for them. They don't believe they will be healed. But, you have enough faith for both of you. Will they be healed?

(Remember that God gives everyone free will. You have probably heard the term "the will to live." If a person doesn't have the "will to live" God will <u>usually</u> not ignore their will and make them live anyway. There is a big difference between someone not believing God *will* heal them and not believing God *can* heal them. Just like there is a big difference between someone not having the faith to believe in what God has to offer and someone not wanting what God has to offer.)

2) Does God really heal people?

(Absolutely. Jesus has already paid the price for your healing... **"by His stripes you are healed." Isaiah 53:5.** If God never healed anyone, then Jesus would have been beaten for nothing. Do you think that God would have let His Son been beaten for nothing?)

3) Aren't Jesus and His twelve disciples the only ones God heals through?

(No! He can heal people using your hands and your prayers if you are a believer of Jesus. **"These signs will follow those who believe... they will lay hands on the sick and they will recover." Mark 16:17,18)**

Activity

Directions: Do you have any illnesses or disabilities that you want God to heal? Or maybe you have a relative or a friend who needs healing? Write down whatever it is on this paper. Don't worry, you don't have to show anyone. You can fold it and stick it in your pocket if you want. God can still see it. Now, pray with your classmates about it. And pray about the things your friends need too. Most of all have faith that God loves you enough to answer your prayer with healing.

Here are a few promises of God on the subject of healing. If you prayed with your class about someone you love that needs healing, you should share these scriptures with them too.

But to you who fear My Name The Sun of Righteousness shall arise with healing in His wings... Malachi 4:2

O Lord My God, I cried to You and You have healed me. O Lord, You brought my soul up from the grave; You have kept me alive, that I should not go down to the pit. Psalm 30:2,3

The Lord will strengthen him on his bed of illness; You will sustain him on his sickbed. Psalm 41:3

He sent His word and healed them, And delivered them from their destructions. Psalm 107:20

Miracles

Lesson Forty-One

Scripture of the Week:
But Jesus said, "Do not forbid him, for no one who works a miracle in My name can soon afterward speak evil of Me.

Mark 9:39

Lesson: Have you ever needed a miracle? You are not alone. Fortunately God still does miracles. He often does it through people, not always, but often. The people God does miracles through have the gift of the Spirit called the working of miracles. [1]

Jesus performed more miracles than could even fit in the Bible. But, Jesus was not the only one who God performed miracles through. Moses did them, Samson, Elijah, Isaiah... the list goes on. And there are countless of God's followers today working miracles with the power of the Holy Spirit.

People say "it would take a miracle," as if a miracle is something that just happens every once in a lifetime. But, the truth is, God works miracles all the time. Sometimes things we call a "coincidence" are really miracles of God.

When a tragedy occurs, like a terrorist bombing or an earthquake, you usually only hear about all the lives lost. And everyone questions God. "How could God let something like this happen?" But, do you ever hear about all the miracles that happened too? Do you hear about the guy who was supposed to be at work, but couldn't find his shoes? He looked all over the house and after fifteen minutes of searching he finally found the shoes where he always keeps them. Someone threw a jacket on top of them. Mad, because he is going to be late, he drives like a maniac to get there. Then he turns on the radio and hears that the building he was racing to get to was just blown up? Lots of people are dead. But, because he couldn't find his shoes, he was late. And he lived.

You have probably had a miracle happen to you, whether you realize it or not. And, whether you realize it or not, you are a miracle. But, what happens when you really, really need a miracle?

Then, you pray. You can pray for the miracle you need. But, it is even more important to pray that God's will be done. [2] So, why do we have to pray for God to do His own will? If it is God's will, won't He just do it anyway? Does He need our permission to do what He wants? After all, He is God. He can do it with or without our prayers. Yes and no. Remember that God won't force His will for your life on you. You have a choice... to follow or not to follow God. By praying for God to do His Will, you are, in a way, giving Him permission. What you are really doing is giving Him the lead and telling Him you will follow.

So, what happens if you pray for your miracle, without caring about what God's will is? God won't do anything against His will. But, be careful. God may give you exactly what you prayed for. But, it may not turn out like you expected. Then, next time, you may be a little more willing to pray for His Will to be done.

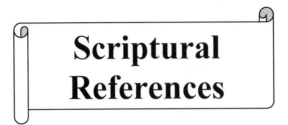

Scriptural References

1   to another the working of miracles, to another prophecy, to another discerning of spirits, to another different kinds of tongues, to another the interpretation of tongues. **1 Corinthians 12:10**

2   **Your kingdom come. Your will be done On earth as it is in heaven.**   Matthew 6:10

Discussion Questions

1) Why does God let bad things happen?
   (No one really knows the answer to this question. There is evil in the world because of the sin. God didn't cause the evil, the sin did. But, no one really knows how many bad things God prevents from happening either. And sometimes God allows us to go through bad times so we learn to count on Him, instead of ourselves.)

2) How can you be a miracle? People make babies all the time.
   (People don't make babies. God does. Remember that God created mankind to be able to reproduce. But, God provides all the miraculous things necessary for a new life to be formed... and He adds the spirit.)

3) Can only Jesus and His original twelve disciples work miracles?
   (God really does the work. But, He often does it through people who are believers in Christ. Jesus' disciples saw someone they did not know casting out demons in Jesus' Name. Because he was not one of their group, they told him not to do it. But, Jesus corrected them. He told them, **"Do not forbid him, for no one who works a miracle in My name can soon afterward speak evil of Me." Mark 9:38, 39.** That shows that you don't have to be Jesus or one of His first twelve disciples to work miracles in Jesus' name.)

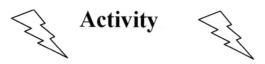 # Activity

Directions: Do you, or someone you know, <u>really need</u> a miracle. Write down what you think you (or they) need here. Pray about it. See if you can find a promise of God relating to it and write that down here too. Keep on praying and believing until you feel you have received an answer from God. Remember sometimes the miracle we <u>think</u> we need, turns out to be different than the miracle we <u>really need.</u>

Or

Write a story about someone who <u>really</u> needed a miracle, prayed for it, believed for it, and received it.

Knowledge

Lesson Forty-Two

Scripture of the Week:
If you seek her as silver, And search for her as for hidden treasures; Then you will understand the fear of the Lord, And find the knowledge of God.

Psalm 2:4,5

Lesson: Wow. A gift of knowledge from the Holy Spirit... now you don't have to worry about figuring out fractions anymore. You wish. Sorry, but it isn't that kind of knowledge. Remember that the gifts of the Holy Spirit are mainly to encourage the church... not to help with homework. You'll have to pray a little differently for that kind of knowledge. (Wouldn't it be nice to have "fruit of the fractions" from the Holy Spirit?)

Imagine a new girl just got to your school. She looks lonely. So, you decide to make friends with her. You introduce yourself and start talking to her about what you'll be doing this weekend. You are just about to tell her about something special you are going to do for your mom Sunday for Mother's Day, but you suddenly stop yourself. It was if someone just whispered in your ear... "Don't say it! Her mother just died recently and this is the first Mother's Day without her." So, you steer the conversation to church instead. Your youth group is going to play miniature golf Saturday afternoon. You invite her to go along. She said she would ask her dad. After you tell her good bye, as you are walking away, under your breath you say a quick prayer for your new friend. One day, you decide, you will pray with her, not just for her.

This is an example of the gift of knowledge. The Holy Spirit will give you a little bit of information about someone, whatever He needs you to know so that you will know how to pray for someone or what to or what not to say to them.

The gift of knowledge is also given to bring people into the Kingdom of God. God sometimes reveals knowledge about a person's past that only He and that person knows. That shows them how real God is. For example, maybe Timmy thinks it is his fault that his parents got divorced, because he heard them argue with each other once about him not cleaning his room. They got divorced right afterward. But, Timmy was ashamed and never told anyone what he thought was a deep dark secret. But, then one day Johnny started talking to Timmy and received a word of knowledge from God. Johnny told Timmy, "You have always blamed yourself for your parent's divorce, but you had nothing to do with it. They were arguing about everything those days and had already decided to get a divorce." Timmy is amazed and relieved. He has carried guilt around for years. Now he wants to know how Johnny knew about his feelings. And Johnny introduces Timmy to the Holy Spirit, Jesus, and God.

But, the Holy Spirit respects privacy. He is not going to tell you something that will embarrass someone. Although, He may use you to let the person know that he has something to be embarrassed about, without clueing you in to what it is. And He won't tell you anything about sins God has forgiven someone. Forgiven sins are in the past and that is where they stay. Jesus took care of that for us. [1] So, the Holy Spirit certainly isn't going to bring those up again.

People God chooses to give the gift of knowledge to are like the people He chooses to give the other gifts of the Holy Spirit to. They want the gift and they pray for it. [2] But, they are also followers that God trusts to do His work. He knows their hearts and makes sure they are in the right place before giving them the gift.

Of course, sometimes a person with a gift of the Holy Spirit forgets the gifts are to encourage the church. Or they forget they are supposed to be acting like Jesus. But, you can always tell them by their fruit. [3] Remember that the fruits of the Spirit are love, joy, peace, patience, gentleness, goodness, kindness, faith, and self-control. Jesus tells us that a good tree makes good fruit and a bad tree makes bad fruit. [4] So, be sure the tree is good before you trust its fruit.

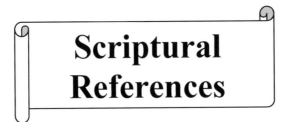

Scriptural References

1   And you, being dead in your trespasses and the uncircumcision of your flesh, He has made alive together with Him, having forgiven you all trespasses, having wiped out the handwriting of requirements that was against us, which was contrary to us. And He has taken it out of the way, having nailed it to the cross. Colossians 2:13-14

2   Then you will understand the fear of the LORD, And find the knowledge of God. For the LORD gives wisdom; From His mouth come knowledge and understanding; Proverbs 2:5,6

3   "For every tree is known by its own fruit. For men do not gather figs from thorns, nor do they gather grapes from a bramble bush. Luke 6:44

4   "Even so, every good tree bears good fruit, but a bad tree bears bad fruit. Matthew 7:17

Discussion Questions

1) How does the gift of knowledge help the church?

(It helps you know what to pray for people. If someone comes to you and needs healing, because their foot hurts, but they don't know why, a word of knowledge from God helps. You start praying for them and God shows you that this person has a bone spur that needs to be removed by the doctor. They had no idea they had a bone spur and aside from that word of knowledge, it would have taken an X-ray to find the bone spur. Maybe they just thought they had pulled a muscle and had no plans to see the doctor.)

2) How can a person have gifts of the Spirit, like knowledge without having the fruit of the Spirit, like love?

(A gift is something that God gives to you, for free. Its purpose is to build and encourage His church. A fruit is something that must be grown. God plants the seed of love in you before you are born, but you have to care for it and help it grow. Sometimes people forget how important the fruits are. They don't water it. And you know what happens to a plant if you don't water it. It certainly doesn't grow fruit.)

Activity

Directions: "Decode" the message.
The underlined words are answers to the puzzle.

My <u>son,</u> if <u>you</u> receive my <u>words,</u>
And <u>treasure</u> my <u>commands</u> within<u>,</u>
<u>So</u> that you <u>incline</u> your <u>ear to</u> wisdom,
And <u>apply</u> your <u>heart to</u> understanding;
Yes, if you <u>cry</u> out <u>for</u> discernment,
And lift <u>up</u> your voice <u>for understanding</u>
If <u>you</u> seek her as <u>silver,</u>
And search <u>for</u> her as *for* hidden <u>treasures;</u>
Then you will understand the <u>fear</u> of the Lord,
And find the knowledge of God.

Proverbs 2:1-5

Wisdom

Lesson Forty-Three

Scripture of the Week:
Wisdom is the principal thing; therefore get wisdom. And in all your getting, get understanding.

Proverbs 4:7

Lesson: Isn't wisdom something old people are supposed to have? Well, who is older than God? Imagine having a bit of God's wisdom. Wow!

Sometimes God doesn't want to wait until we get as old as grandpa to have some wisdom. Besides, how many kids do you know who, when they are faced with a tough decision like whether or not to cheat on their math test, go and ask grandpa advice? Yeah, right. Wouldn't you like to be the person to help keep your friends out of trouble?

The gift of wisdom helps you think about the things that your friends might not think about. . Sure, you can go through all the things they know, cheating is wrong... yada yada yada. Maybe they are listening. Maybe they aren't. But, what happens if they get caught cheating on the test? You remind them that you are having a slumber party next weekend. Don't think mom's going to let them go if they cheat on that test. "Oh yeah. Hadn't thought of that." That may be all the motivation they need to forget the whole cheating idea.

Of course, the gift of wisdom can help in other ways too. You may have just met a really mean substitute teacher. People in the back row are already wadding up spitballs. But, you being full of wisdom from the Spirit of God, you realize that she isn't really mean. She is shy and a little scared facing all of these kids. She thinks that if she appears tough, the kids will behave. So, you are nice to her. And you tell those other kids, "How would you feel if you had to sit up in front of a bunch of kids you don't know and they started shooting spit balls at you." A few of the kids put down their spitballs, ashamed. But, one kid readies his aim. The boy who sits behind him, one who had a spit ball of his own a minute before, says, "John, don't be a jerk." Suddenly, it is no longer cool to be a jerk. He puts down his straw.

Your friend comes to you for advice. Her parents are divorced. They both want her to spend Christmas with them, but they live in two different cities. They have left the decision up to her. She doesn't know what to do. You start giving her some very good advice. You explain to her how her parents are probably feeling and how she can find a solution that will satisfy everyone. She thanks you for your help... amazed at the wisdom of your solution. You are amazed too. "Where did that come from?" you think to yourself. Your parents are happily married. How would you know what to do? You didn't. God does. You just saw the gift of wisdom in action.

Like all of the other gifts of the Spirit, the gift of wisdom can help with the really big stuff too... major life changes like divorce, moving, finding a new job, switching schools,

death of a loved one. God has an answer for everything that can happen to you. [1] Those with true wisdom know where to look for those answers. Life isn't easy. But, God makes finding His answers easy. He keeps them all in one book... the Bible. [2]

Never think that because you are young that you can't have wisdom. God is not a respecter of persons. [3] That means, he doesn't look at your age any more than he looks at the color of your skin or which bathroom you have to use at the mall. God is concerned with your heart. [4] Some of God's greatest followers began making a difference as children. Samuel was a minister before God when he was still a child. David, a future king of Israel, took down a giant as a boy. Even Jesus thanked God saying, "You have hidden these things from the wise and prudent and have revealed them to babes." [5]

There are as many different ways the gift of wisdom can help, as there are prayers that need to be said. Listen closely to God. He has enough wisdom for the entire world. [6]

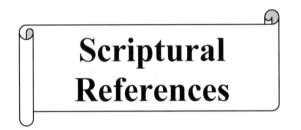

Scriptural References

1   Have you heard the counsel of God? Do you limit wisdom to yourself? Job 15:8

2   Then those who feared the LORD spoke to one another, And the LORD listened and heard them; So a book of remembrance was written before Him For those who fear the LORD And who meditate on His name. Malachi 3:16

3   Then Peter opened his mouth and said: "In truth I perceive that God shows no partiality. But in every nation whoever fears Him and works righteousness is accepted by Him." Acts 10:34,35

4   Would not God search this out? For He knows the secrets of the heart. Psalm 44:21

5   At that time Jesus answered and said, "I thank You, Father, Lord of heaven and earth, that You have hidden these things from the wise and prudent and have revealed them to babes. Matthew 11:25

6   Because the foolishness of God is wiser than men, and the weakness of God is stronger than men. 1 Corinthians 1:25

Discussion Questions

1) How does the gift of wisdom help the church?

(You are borrowing a small part of the wisdom of God. By sharing that wisdom you can help people make good decisions.)

2) Won't people think you are a "know it all" if you are walking around handing out God's wisdom?

(It all depends on how you go about it. Have you ever had a friend ask you for advice and then call you a know-it-all when you give her some? Probably not. If you offer advice with a humble spirit (gentle and very un-know-it-all like), it is usually well received.)

3) So, when you tell someone what you feel is from the Holy Spirit, do you tell them it came from God?

(Just tell them the truth. Tell them that you believe it is from the Holy Spirit. If you are not sure, then tell them you are not sure. If it does not agree with the Bible... it isn't from the Holy Spirit and isn't something you should be passing off as good advice anyway.)

4) What if someone asks you for advice and you really don't have a clue what to tell them?

(That is when you both go on a scripture hunt... together if possible. Tell your friend, "I really don't know, but let's see what God has to say about this. Use the index (concordance) in the back of the Bible to help you find what you are looking for. One of the best things in the world you can do for someone is to teach them to seek God's advice on things.)

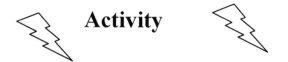

Activity

Directions: Name as many things as you can think of that someone your age can do to help the kingdom of God grow?

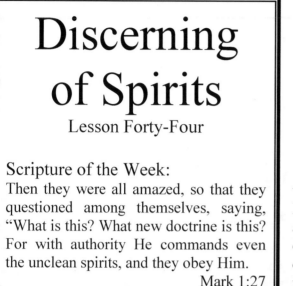

Discerning of Spirits

Lesson Forty-Four

Scripture of the Week:

Then they were all amazed, so that they questioned among themselves, saying, "What is this? What new doctrine is this? For with authority He commands even the unclean spirits, and they obey Him.

Mark 1:27

Lesson: The devil and his evil spirits today cause most of the bad things in the world. If someone is being a jerk to you, chances are an evil spirit is motivating them. Demon spirits often causes illness, disease, and mental disorders, too. Sometimes these spirits live inside the people, sometimes they have attached themselves to them, and sometimes they are just attacking. Not every illness, disease, mental disorder, or person acting like a jerk is a demon spirit. That is where having the ability to discern spirits helps.

The gift, another of the gifts of the Holy Spirit, allows you to tell if there is a demon spirit present, or if it is something else causing the problem. If you determine that it is a demon spirit, then you can cast it out or rebuke it in the Name of Jesus.

When Jesus walked the earth, He cast out demons all the time. A man at the edge of town that was chained up and left in a cemetery was thought to be crazy. But, Jesus knew he was demon-possessed. That means that demons lived inside him. Jesus cast out the demons and the man was just fine. He went home to his family who was astonished. [1] Jesus cast the demons out of a blind man who couldn't talk. Suddenly, the man's sight came back and he was able to speak again. [2] Even after Jesus went on to heaven, His disciples continued to cast out spirits. [3] Jesus told us that His followers would cast out demons in His name. [4] That means you, too. If you are a follower and believer of Jesus, then you have the authority, in Christ, to cast out demons.

But, if you are not, don't try it. Some men who weren't followers of Christ tried it. They announced to the demons, "We exorcise you by the Jesus whom Paul preaches." But, the demon answered him, "Jesus I know, and Paul I know; but who are you?" Then the man who was demon-possessed jumped on them, beat them up and sent them running off naked. [5]

Although, you can cast out demons (as long as you are truly one of God's) without the ability to discern spirits, it is much easier with it. When you tell a spirit, "Come out in the name of Jesus!" it is also helpful to say the spirit's name. Their name is usually the same as what it is they do to a person. In other words, if you have a friend that is very afraid of something, she is probably being attacked by the spirit of fear. You can rebuke it (tell it to go away) by saying, "I rebuke the spirit of fear in the name of Jesus!" If you feel it is living inside her add, "Spirit of fear, come out of her in the name of Jesus!" If you are the one who is afraid, just tell it to "Go away, in the name of Jesus!" The Name of Jesus alone... just His Name... is more powerful than any demon or devil.

The gift of discerning spirits is not just the ability to pick out the evil ones. You will also be able to tell when someone has a sweet spirit, too. You will be able to tell God's own.[6] But, if they are true followers of Jesus, walking in His ways, you won't need a gift of the Spirit to do that. You will be able to tell; just by the way they act.

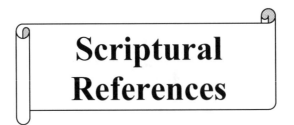

Scriptural References

1 And when He had come out of the boat, immediately there met Him out of the tombs a man with an unclean spirit, who had his dwelling among the tombs; and no one could bind him, not even with chains, For He said to him, "Come out of the man, unclean spirit!" Then they came to Jesus, and saw the one who had been demon-possessed and had the legion, sitting and clothed and in his right mind. And they were afraid. And he departed and began to proclaim in Decapolis all that Jesus had done for him; and all marveled.   Mark 5:2,3,8,15,20

2 Then one was brought to Him who was demon-possessed, blind and mute; and He healed him, so that the blind and mute man both spoke and saw. Matthew 12:22

3 And this she did for many days. But Paul, greatly annoyed, turned and said to the spirit, "I command you in the name of Jesus Christ to come out of her." And he came out that very hour.   Acts 16:18

4 "And these signs will follow those who believe: In My name they will cast out demons; they will speak with new tongues; Mark 16:17

5 And the evil spirit answered and said, "Jesus I know, and Paul I know; but who are you?" Then the man in whom the evil spirit was leaped on them, overpowered them, and prevailed against them, so that they fled out of that house naked and wounded. Acts 19:15,16

6 Then you shall again discern Between the righteous and the wicked, Between one who serves God And one who does not serve Him. Malachi 3:18

Discussion Questions

1) Can a person be demon possessed and Spirit-filled (having the Holy Spirit living inside them) at the same time?

(No. Evil cannot exist in the presence of God. And the Holy Spirit is the presence of God in you. But, demon spirits do try to attack Spirit-filled people by trying to tempt them to sin.)

2) Are demon-possessed people like what you see in the scary movies?

(Not usually. What happens is that normal people sometimes unknowingly invite an evil spirit to live in them. That evil spirit often controls a person's free will and clouds their judgment. The demon is in control)

3) What are some ways a person invites a spirit to live in them?

(Sin opens the door for demons to move right in. Sin is anything that is against God. They are especially attracted to ...people experimenting with the occult (Ouiji boards, tarot cards, palm readers, etc.), demonic and cursed objects, (especially things that represent worship to a false God, like a buddha statue or Egyptian Ahnks)

4) Can you have more than one evil spirit living in you at once?

(Yes. When Jesus met the man in the cemetery, the demons in him called themselves "Legion" because there were so many of them.)

5) How can you protect yourself from demons and keep them from trying to attach or move in with you?

(Don't sin, would be the obvious answer. But, also make sure that you don't have occult or demonic items in your home. One of the devil's latest tricks is to get people to buy demonic toys. These are usually action figures in the shape of hideous monsters and creatures. Jewelry, comic books, posters, books, and even music have been known to attract demonic spirits. A discerning spirit will help pick out what shouldn't be in your home. But, if you start looking at things as if you are looking through the eyes of Jesus that will help you get rid of the evil stuff.)

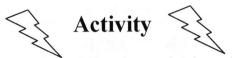 **Activity**

Directions: Can you match up which spirits are operating in each story?

1) spirit of jealousy   4) spirit of the fear of rejection
2) spirit of fear   5) spirit of the antichrist and pride
3) spirit of division

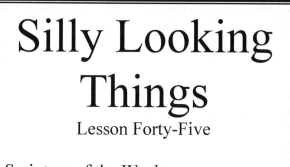

Silly Looking Things

Lesson Forty-Five

Scripture of the Week:
But God has chosen the foolish things of the world to confound the wise; and God has chosen the weak things of the world to confound the things which are mighty.

1 Corinthians 1:27

Lesson: Have you ever been in church and saw some really strange stuff? The pastor calls up people who want to be prayed for, he lays hands on them and starts praying. The next thing you know, people are hitting the floor, dropping like flies. Maybe one or two of them start giggling uncontrollably. And then you have a few "shakers" that keep looking like they want to fall, but never do? What on earth is all of this?

These people have received a touch of God.[1] God is so awesome that a little touch from Him can make us do some weird things. But, God knows what He is doing, even if we don't. And He knows just what you need when you need it.

Those people on the floor, well, maybe that is the only way God can get us still long enough to spend some quality time with Him. The gigglers? Well, they probably needed a touch of the joy of the Lord. And the shakers? Who knows what God is doing there? He says He confounds the wise with foolishness.[2] So, maybe He is just keeping people humble. So, do you have to fall or shake or laugh? No. The Holy Spirit isn't going to force you to do anything. But, if you are willing to receive what the Lord has for you, and He has a touch in mind, you could be the next one doing "silly stuff."

What does it feel like? It is a little different for everyone. During these times God may be healing, teaching, comforting, filling with joy or whatever else you need. You may feel a sensation of warmth or peace. You may feel relief, as worry just floats away. Or you may even feel kind of light, like you are floating on a cloud. Whatever you feel, you will feel that you have been touched by God.

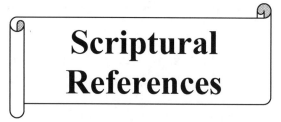

Scriptural References

[1] **"And it shall come to pass afterward That I will pour out My Spirit on all flesh; Your sons and your daughters shall prophesy, Your old men shall dream dreams, Your young men shall see visions. Joel 2:28**

2 **But God has chosen the foolish things of the world to put to shame the wise, and God has chosen the weak things of the world to put to shame the things which are mighty; 1 Corinthians 1:27**

Discussion Questions

1) Does the Bible tell us about "going out in the Spirit" and other "silly looking things?"

(Paul of Tarsus met Jesus on the way to Damascus. He hit the dirt. Later, he was praying in the temple and went into what he described as a "trance." (Acts 22: 7,17)

When the disciples were first filled with the Holy Spirit, people accused them of being drunk because of the way they were acting. (Acts 2:15)

King David, who danced often to the Lord, said, "You will make me full of joy in Your presence. (Acts 2:28). That would certainly explain the giggles.)

2) Is going out in the Spirit really real?

(Thousands of people could tell you it is. But, once you experience it for yourself, you will never doubt again.)

3) Why do people want to get up in front of everyone and look so silly?

(People who have experienced or want to experience a touch from God are more interested in being close to Him than looking "dignified" to other people.)

 **Activity**

If you, or someone else who is available, could pray over the children to let them experience a "touch from God" this would be a perfect time. But since we can't schedule moves of the Holy Spirit an alternative activity is included.

Directions: Name all the "silly" looking things you have seen people do and why they do them. Which of these things don't seem silly unless you see people do them in church?

Why do you think things that usually look fine where people do them (like jumping up and down at a football game) seem very strange if they are done in church?

Witnessing to the World By Your Actions

Lesson Forty-Six

Scripture of the Week:

Let no one despise your youth, but be an example to the believers in word, in conduct, in love, in spirit, in faith, in purity.

1 Timothy 4:12

Lesson: Let your Jesus show. The Lord tells us to **"let our light so shine before men that they may see your good works and glorify your Father in heaven."** [1] So what exactly does that mean? If you are a follower of Christ, a true believer, then, it should show. If you have Jesus living in your heart, the people around you should be able to tell, just by your actions.

You are an ambassador for Christ. There are many ambassadors from other countries living in the United States. If the ambassador from England shoplifted, got drunk, and got into fist fights while at some party for the president, how would that make England look? If their ambassador, who is supposed to be England's representative to the world, is that bad, how much worse are the ones they kept in England? Americans would start to think that all the English were trouble making, lawbreaking, drunks. Not a pretty picture.

If you are a Christian, you are a representative of the Kingdom of God. How do you want to represent King Jesus? If you lie to your parents, make fun of the unpopular kids in school, be mean to your little brother, and cuss like a sailor... how does that make your King look? People will look and say; "Those Christians are a bunch of hypocrites. They preach to love one another, but look at how they act. You can't turn your back on them, they will stab you in it." Not a pretty picture.

Before you do something you shouldn't... think about how it would look. How will you be representing the Kingdom if you cheat on that test?

But, if you follow Jesus, and let Him shine in your life, now that is a pretty picture. Let your Jesus show. Go out of your way to help people, speak kindly, love everyone, be a joy to others. Put God first. People will notice. And without saying a word, you will become a great ambassador, a wonderful witness of Jesus. You never know how many people will turn their lives over to Jesus because they can see Him in you. And they will want what you have. Don't be surprised if people ask you to pray for them or start asking you questions about God. If they do, you will know that you are doing a good job as ambassador to the King.

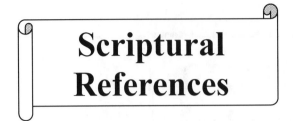

Scriptural References

1 "Let your light so shine before men, that they may see your good works and glorify your Father in heaven. Matthew 5:16

Discussion Questions

1) When you "let your Jesus show" won't people think you are just a nice person? How will they know that it is Jesus in you?

(When you are a follower of Jesus, and you love Him, you can't help but talk about Him. You don't have to preach to people. But, if they see you pray before meals, thank God for all the little things as well as the big things, and quote the Bible, they will begin to get the picture. If you spend time learning about what God has to say to us in His Bible, you can't help but quote Him. Eventually it will come naturally.)

2) But, won't people call you a "Jesus freak" and learn to avoid you?

(Many people died because they wanted a title like that. But, just like anything, if you talk to some people about one subject too long, it will turn people off. If all Mark ever talked about what monster truck rallies... and you had about all of the monster truck rally conversations you could stand... you would probably avoid Mark. But, if you loved monster truck rallies, you would probably never get tired of hearing about them from Mark. Talking about Jesus is similar. If you know someone that really loves Jesus... you can talk and talk to them about Jesus. But, if you are trying to introduce someone to Jesus, take it slow. You don't want to turn them off before you turn them on to Him. That doesn't mean you are ashamed of the gospel of Christ. That means you are using wisdom in how you introduce someone to Christ. Let your love for Jesus show, but consider the person you are talking to. Let the Holy Spirit show you the best way to reveal the love of Christ to them... then go for it!)

⚡ Activity ⚡

Directions: Are you being a good ambassador for Christ? Take a little quiz to see how you are doing. Be perfectly honest with your answers. Don't just choose what you think is the "right" answer. Choose what you <u>really do</u>. No one will see this quiz, unless you decide to show it to them.

Witnessing to the World Friends and Family

Lesson Forty-Seven

Scripture of the Week:
And let us not grow weary while doing good, for in due season we shall reap if we do not lose heart.

Galatians 6:9

Lesson: What happens if you find that you are the only one of your friends that is a Christian? Do you ditch them and make new friends? Or do you stick with them and try to turn them on to Christ? What if you are the only one in your family that is a Christian? You can't exactly ditch your family.

The Lord tells us not to be unevenly yoked with unbelievers.[1] A yoke is like a harness. They put yokes on animals, like oxen when they are working, so it will be easier to get them to work together. Picture this... you have two oxen hooked together with steel and leather. They have no choice in the matter. They are basically slaves to whatever their master wants them to do. They can't just walk away or quit whenever they want... kind of the ox's version of a gang. This is what God is trying to save you from. If you become yoked with unbelievers, you become like a slave, doing whatever the unbeliever is doing. And remember the unbeliever's master is the devil. You want no part of that.

But, wait a minute. Jesus hung out with the unbelievers didn't He? Didn't the chief priests and Pharisees, the so-called holy men of their time, get all mad at Jesus for hanging out with the rebels?[2] Jesus made friends with the tax collectors and the harlots... definitely unbelievers. Remember that Jesus came to call the sinners, not the righteous, to repentance.[3] It wouldn't have done anyone any good if He hung out with the righteous all the time and avoided the sinners. But, Jesus never became "yoked" with them. He never became like them or did anything they did. He taught them His ways. And most of them were thrilled to hear all about it. They repented from their evil ways and became disciples of Jesus. Sounds like they became yoked with Jesus, instead of the other way around. Jesus said, "Take My yoke upon you and learn from Me, for I am gentle and lowly in heart, and you will find rest for your souls. For My yoke is easy and My burden is light."[4]

So what about the unbelievers who still do not want to believe? Jesus tells us, "Whoever will not receive you or hear your words, when you depart from them, shake the dust off your feet."[5] In other words, don't let it trouble you. You are called to spread the Word of God, not to argue with people who don't want to believe. This is when you need to prayerfully consider if you are hanging out with the right crowd.

So, what do you do if it is your close friend or family that doesn't believe? First, make sure you tell them the good news of Jesus. But, don't argue and don't become a broken record, repeating and repeating and repeating yourself. This is when letting your Jesus show really counts. Living your believe in front of them is the best way to win them over to God. This means that you definitely do not become yoked with them. But, you show them how much better life is with Jesus.

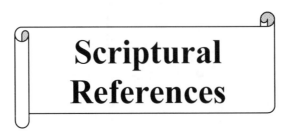

Scriptural References

1   **Do not be unequally yoked together with unbelievers. For what fellowship has righteousness with lawlessness? And what communion has light with darkness? And what accord has Christ with Belial? Or what part has a believer with an unbeliever? Therefore "Come out from among them And be separate, says the Lord. Do not touch what is unclean, And I will receive you." 2 Corinthians 6:14,15,17**

2   **And when the Pharisees saw it, they said to His disciples, "Why does your Teacher eat with tax collectors and sinners?" Matthew 9:11**

3   **"But go and learn what this means: 'I desire mercy and not sacrifice.' For I did not come to call the righteous, but sinners, to repentance." Matthew 9:13**

4   **"Take My yoke upon you and learn from Me, for I am gentle and lowly in heart, and you will find rest for your souls. "For My yoke is easy and My burden is light." Matthew 11:29,30**

5   **"And whoever will not receive you nor hear your words, when you depart from that house or city, shake off the dust from your feet. Matthew 10:14**

Discussion Questions

1) What is the yoke of Jesus?

(Jesus expects us to love on another. If you truly love, you will automatically follow the rest of God's commandments.)

2) What is the line between being yoked with an unbeliever and witnessing to unbelievers?

(Your heart is the line, which is shown in your actions. If you start sinning like the unbeliever, you have become yoked with him. But, if you teach the ways of Jesus to him, without starting to sin like him, you are witnessing. You need to be very careful. The Lord warns us to **"come out from among them and be separate. Do not touch what is unclean, And I will receive you. 2 Corinthians 6:17**. If you are the light of the world, you have no business hanging out with something that can extinguish your flame.)

3) Are you responsible for another's salvation?

(No. People have to work out their own salvation. But, you are held responsible for telling them about Jesus. **"Go into all the world and preach the gospel to every creature. He who believes and is baptized will be saved; but he who does not believe will be condemned."** **Mark 16:15,16.** That tells us to simply tell people about the gospel of Jesus. The choice to accept or reject Christ is entirely theirs.)

4) What do you do if you have told someone about Jesus and "let your Jesus show," but they still reject Christ?

(Pray that their blinders be removed so they may see the truth. And, in the Name of Jesus, bind up the deceiving spirits that are coming against them. Then keep praying for their salvation. That is the best thing you can do for them.)

Activity

Directions: Pretend that you are the only Christian in your group of friends or in your family. You want your loved ones to join you in heaven one day. In the hopes that they too will turn their lives over to Christ, you realize you must really "let your Jesus show." Write and act out a skit of someone witnessing to their friends or family by "letting their Jesus show."

(**Teacher note**: Divide the class into smaller groups and give them a time limit, for example five to ten minutes, to complete their skits. Then let them act them out.)

Missions

Lesson Forty-Eight

Scripture of the Week:
Go therefore and make disciples of all the nations, baptizing them in the name of the Father and of the Son and of the Holy Spirit.

Matthew 28:19

Lesson: "Go therefore and make **disciples of all the nations, baptizing them in the name of the Father and of the Son and of the Holy Spirit, teaching them to observe <u>all</u> things that I have commanded you; and lo, I am with you always, even to the end of the age."** [1] Jesus gave all of His believers a great commission. He told us to spread His teachings to the ends of the earth. This was the beginning of missionary work.

Maybe when you think of missionaries you picture people digging ditches in some far off village of Africa. That would be an example of people carrying out foreign missions. Of course, there are missions right here in our own country. You may have heard of churches running soup kitchens or homeless shelters in some of the poorest sections of cities.

Have you ever wondered why they are digging and serving food? Aren't they supposed to be spreading the gospel of Christ? What does digging a ditch or cooking up ten pounds of mashed potatoes have to do with Jesus? Everything.

Jesus said, "If you give food or drink or clothing to one of My brothers, you have done it for me." [2] Missionaries are not just *telling* people about the love of God. They are *showing* them the love of God.

What good would it do to go all the way to Africa and tell some starving family all about the wonderful things of Christ? If their bellies are growling and they haven't eaten for two days, they probably aren't listening to what you have to say anyway. But, if you give them food, and then show them how to work the land so they can grow food for themselves, you have their attention. They will want to know why you came thousands of miles just to feed strangers. That is when you can teach them about all that Christ has to offer.

What about here in America? Surely everyone has heard about Jesus. Not necessarily. Besides, hearing about Jesus and actually knowing Jesus are not the same thing. What about the girl who grew up in an alcoholic home? The abuse was so bad, she ran away and is living on the streets. Maybe no one has ever shown her love. Her life has been one tragedy after another. So, what would make her think that Jesus cares anything about her? No one else has. But, then she meets a local missionary. Instead of just giving her a meal and sending her on her way, he takes the time to get to know her. He convinces her to start spending a little time in the shelter, talking to the counselors and learning about Christ. Before you know it, she has her life turned around, all because a missionary let the love of Jesus shine through him.

Not everyone has a calling to be a foreign missionary. It takes special gifts from God to carry out His service that way. But, we were all given the job to teach the world about Jesus and to spread His Word.

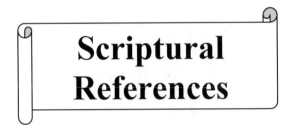

Scriptural References

1   "Go therefore and make disciples of all the nations, baptizing them in the name of the Father and of the Son and of the Holy Spirit, "teaching them to observe all things that I have commanded you; and lo, I am with you always, even to the end of the age." Amen. Matthew 28:19,20

2   "And the King will answer and say to them, 'Assuredly, I say to you, inasmuch as you did it to one of the least of these My brethren, you did it to Me.' Matthew 25:40

Discussion Questions

1) How do missionaries know where to go?
    (They are led by the Holy Spirit wherever God needs them to be.)

2) How can you help the ministries of missionaries?
    (You can go on a mission yourself... to a foreign country or in your own town. You can pray for them. You can give a gift of money, or food, or clothing, or whatever they need.)

3) How do you know if you have a calling to be a missionary?
    (God will put a desire in your heart. Have you ever felt a strong desire to travel to exotic... or not so exotic places? Do you like to work with your hands, doing things

outside, like building or painting or digging? Do you feel a special love and compassion in your heart for the needy... that makes you want to help one on one, instead of just giving money to help? Not only will God put a desire in your heart, but, if you make a commitment to fulfill what God has in mind for you... God will make sure you have the opportunity to go on missions.)

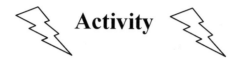

Activity

Directions: Contact a missionary organization and "adopt" a missionary kid. Write to him or her, send pictures, learn about their life and maybe even send them a care package.

OR

Write a story about a kid your age who goes on a missionary trip (with parents, youth group, etc).

Is the Devil Real?

Lesson Forty-Nine

Scripture of the Week:
Above all, taking the shield of faith with which you will be able to quench all the fiery darts of the wicked one.
Ephesians 6:16

Lesson: Is the devil real? He would sure like you to think he wasn't. Then, he could get away with all his tricks and traps and you wouldn't even have a clue where it was coming from. And, if you didn't know that it was the devil doing these things, you sure couldn't stop him.

He comes to kill, steal, and destroy. [1] One of the devil's favorite ways to do that is to deceive (fool) you. He likes to try to deceive people into thinking that the bad stuff in life comes from God. No sir. And if he can make you think there isn't even a devil, all the better to fool you with, my dear.

So, how do you know there is a devil? Look around. Look at all the evil in the world. Remember that you will know whether a tree is good or bad by its fruit. [2] And that devil is one bad apple.

The Bible warns us of our enemy, the devil. The devil isn't like God, he can't be everywhere at once. But, he has an army of followers to help him with his destruction. [3] They are all considered "the enemy." The Bible warns us that the enemy may try to fool us by transforming himself into an angel of light. [4] Or he may even disguise himself as a minister of Christ. [5] Remember that the devil wants those who belong to Jesus. He already has the ones who don't. He will lie, cheat, and steal to get his way. No trick is too dirty, no act too evil. But, you don't have to be afraid of him.

Au contraire, mon frere! If you are a Christian, he has every reason to be afraid of you. You have the authority and ability to crush his evil little head. When Christ died on that cross and rose again, He triumphed over the devil. Jesus beat the devil. He took the keys of death and hell away from him. That means the devil is defeated. [6] He has no authority over you. But, you, belonging to Jesus, have authority over him. [7] Resist the devil and he will flee. [8] Rebuke him in the name of Jesus and he will flee a little faster. Start praising God and he will flee as fast as those claws will carry him.

Scriptural References

1   "The thief does not come except to steal, and to kill, and to destroy. I have come that they may have life, and that they may have it more abundantly.   John 10:10

2   "Even so, every good tree bears good fruit, but a bad tree bears bad fruit. Matthew 7:17

3   "Then He will also say to those on the left hand, 'Depart from Me, you cursed, into the everlasting fire prepared for the devil and his angels: Matthew 25:41

4   And no wonder! For Satan himself transforms himself into an angel of light. 2 Corinthians 11:14

5   Therefore it is no great thing if his ministers also transform themselves into ministers of righteousness, whose end will be according to their works. 2 Corinthians 11:15

6   And you, being dead in your trespasses and the uncircumcision of your flesh, He has made alive together with Him, having forgiven you all trespasses, having wiped out the handwriting of requirements that was against us, which was contrary to us. And He has taken it out of the way, having nailed it to the cross. Having disarmed principalities and powers, He made a public spectacle of them, triumphing over them in it.   Colossians 2:13-15

7   Then He called His twelve disciples together and gave them power and authority over all demons, and to cure diseases.   Luke 9:1

8   Therefore submit to God. Resist the devil and he will flee from you.   James 4:7

Discussion Questions

1) Why doesn't the devil want you to know that he exists?

(If you don't know you have an enemy, you won't learn how to stop that enemy.)

2) Why doesn't he want you to know about his army of demons?

(His demons are his spies and carry out his trickery. Have you ever heard of a country that announced that they had spies and terrorists? Again, if you are unaware of the way the devil works, you won't do anything to stop him.)

3) How do we know demons exist?

(Jesus and His followers were often casting out demons. Jesus also told us that His followers would cast out demons in His name. (Mark 16:17)

4) The devil wants you to be afraid of him. And you should be... or should you?

(Without Jesus, the devil would be really scary. But, since Jesus has already triumphed over the devil, as long as you are a follower of Christ, you have authority over the devil too. When you have the authority of Jesus, the devil needs to be afraid of you.)

Activity

Directions: Draw a picture of you crushing the devil's head.

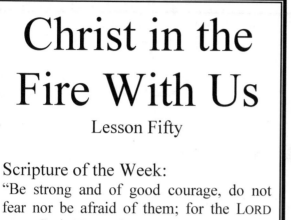

Christ in the Fire With Us

Lesson Fifty

Scripture of the Week:

"Be strong and of good courage, do not fear nor be afraid of them; for the LORD your God, He *is* the One who goes with you. He will not leave you nor forsake you."

Deuteronomy 31:6

Lesson: Bad things happen in the world. That is the way the world is. It didn't start out that way. But, Adam and Eve introduced sin into the world when they ate of the forbidden tree. It has been here ever since. [1] Bad happens to everyone... those who follow God and those who don't. [2] So what good does it do us to be a believer if bad things are going to happen to everyone?

Think of it this way, if you know there is evil in the world, wouldn't you rather have God on your side? There are advantages to belonging to Jesus. If you belong to Him, He will protect you and stay with you throughout the trouble. [3]

Take for example three guys who were God's own. They lived under the rule of a king named Nebuchadnezzar. This King made a statue of gold. Then he ordered everyone to bow down and worship this statue whenever music played. So, when the music played everyone bowed down real quick and started worshipping this piece of metal... except these three guys, Shadrach, Meshach, and Abed-Nego. Some of the metal worshipers ran to the king and told on them. So the king, who was pretty mad at the trio for ignoring his law, sent for the men. He told Shadrach, Meshach and Abed-Nego that they had one more chance to bow down and worship the statue. If they didn't, he would have them thrown into a fiery furnace. Well, the men got an attitude with the king. They told him, "Not only will we not bow down to your supposed God, but our God will save us from you." That really ticked off the king. He instructed his men to turn up the giant oven seven times hotter than usual. Then, they tied up the three men and threw them into the fire. It was so hot, that it killed the guys who threw Shadrach, Meshach, and Abed-Nego into the oven. Then, the King looked and saw in the flames, not three tied up men burning, but four men walking around in the fire, as if they were out for a stroll on the beach. The fourth Man, they said, looked like the Son of God. Immediately, the king ordered the men out of the furnace. Shadrach, Meshach, and Abed-Nego were not only fine; they didn't even smell like smoke. The only thing that had burned was the rope that had tied them. You can bet the king sure changed his attitude towards God. [4]

God didn't keep those guys from being thrown into the fire. But, He did protect them while they were in it. And He was in it with them. He never left them. That's the way God is. He may not always keep bad things from happening. But, He protects His people, and He never leaves them alone to fend for themselves.

We don't know why bad things happen. Although tough situations can help us grow stronger in faith as we learn to put our trust in God, nobody likes to go through rough times. But remember this, Jesus will always be in the fire with you, no matter how hot it gets.

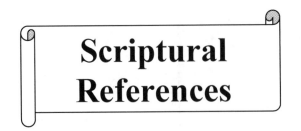

Scriptural References

1   **For as by one man's disobedience many were made sinners, so also by one Man's obedience many will be made righteous.**   **Romans 5:19**

2   **All things come alike to all: One event happens to the righteous and the wicked; To the good, the clean, and the unclean; To him who sacrifices and him who does not sacrifice. As is the good, so is the sinner; He who takes an oath as he who fears an oath.**   **Ecclesiastes 9:2**

3   **"Be strong and of good courage, do not fear nor be afraid of them; for the LORD your God, He is the One who goes with you. He will not leave you nor forsake you." Deuteronomy 31:6**

4   **Therefore at that time certain Chaldeans came forward and accused the Jews. They spoke and said to King Nebuchadnezzar, "O king, live forever! "You, O king, have made a decree that everyone who hears the sound of the horn, flute, harp, lyre, and psaltery, in symphony with all kinds of music, shall fall down and worship the gold image; and whoever does not fall down and worship shall be cast into the midst of a burning fiery furnace. "There are certain Jews whom you have set over the affairs of the province of Babylon: Shadrach, Meshach, and Abed-Nego; these men, O king, have not paid due regard to you. They do not serve your gods or worship the gold image which you have set up."**
    Then Nebuchadnezzar, in rage and fury, gave the command to bring Shadrach, Meshach, and Abed-Nego. So they brought these men before the king. Nebuchadnezzar spoke, saying to them, "Is it true, Shadrach, Meshach, and Abed-Nego, that you do not serve my gods or worship the gold image which I have set up? "Now if you are ready at the time you hear the sound of the horn, flute, harp, lyre, and psaltery, in symphony with all kinds of music, and you fall down and worship the image which I have made, good! But if you do not worship, you shall be cast immediately into the midst of a burning fiery furnace. And who is the god who will deliver you from my hands?"
    Shadrach, Meshach, and Abed-Nego answered and said to the king, "O Nebuchadnezzar, we have no need to answer you in this matter. If that is the case, our God whom we serve is able to deliver us from the burning fiery furnace, and He will deliver us from your hand, O king. But if not, let it be known to you, O king, that we do not serve your gods, nor will we worship the gold image which you have set up."

Then Nebuchadnezzar was full of fury, and the expression on his face changed toward Shadrach, Meshach, and Abed-Nego. He spoke and commanded that they heat the furnace seven times more than it was usually heated. And he commanded certain mighty men of valor who were in his army to bind Shadrach, Meshach, and Abed-Nego, and cast them into the burning fiery furnace. Then these men were bound in their coats, their trousers, their turbans, and their other garments, and were cast into the midst of the burning fiery furnace. Therefore, because the king's command was urgent, and the furnace exceedingly hot, the flame of the fire killed those men who took up Shadrach, Meshach, and Abed-Nego. And these three men, Shadrach, Meshach, and Abed-Nego, fell down bound into the midst of the burning fiery furnace.

Then King Nebuchadnezzar was astonished; and he rose in haste and spoke, saying to his counselors, "Did we not cast three men bound into the midst of the fire?" They answered and said to the king, "True, O king." "Look!" he answered, "I see four men loose, walking in the midst of the fire; and they are not hurt, and the form of the fourth is like the Son of God."

Then Nebuchadnezzar went near the mouth of the burning fiery furnace and spoke, saying, "Shadrach, Meshach, and Abed-Nego, servants of the Most High God, come out, and come here." Then Shadrach, Meshach, and Abed-Nego came from the midst of the fire. And the satraps, administrators, governors, and the king's counselors gathered together, and they saw these men on whose bodies the fire had no power; the hair of their head was not singed nor were their garments affected, and the smell of fire was not on them. Nebuchadnezzar spoke, saying, "Blessed be the God of Shadrach, Meshach, and Abed-Nego, who sent His Angel and delivered His servants who trusted in Him, and they have frustrated the king's word, and yielded their bodies, that they should not serve nor worship any god except their own God!   Daniel 3:8-28

Discussion Questions

1) Why doesn't God just get rid of the bad stuff in the world?

(He plans to. When He created the world, it was perfect. Adam and Eve let sin into the world by eating the forbidden fruit. But, after many things happen, God will make a new heaven and a new earth. God will live with men there. There will be no tears or death or sorrow or pain. (Revelation 21:3,4) There will be no more bad stuff.)

2) Why does God let us go through bad stuff instead of just keeping it away from us?

(We don't know all the reasons God does what He does. But, we do know that hard times can help us learn to count on God. It can make our faith stronger when we learn that God will never leave us. Once you have made it through a tough time, you are not as afraid of the next tough time. Because you know that God will see you through it.)

Activity

Directions: Draw and color a picture of Shadrach, Meshach, and Abed-Nego, with Jesus, in the fiery furnace.

Angels

Lesson Fifty-One

Lesson: Angels have become pretty popular lately. You see images of angels you can wear as jewelry, hang on a wall, or read about in a book. But, have you ever wondered how mankind knows what angels look like?

Angels have appeared to people for almost as long as people have been around. The angel Gabriel appeared to Mary to tell her she would be having Jesus. [1] And he appeared to Zacharias, the father of John the Baptist, to tell him he would also have a son. [2] Angels ministered to Jesus, after the devil tried to tempt Him three times. [3] And an angel appeared to Mary again to tell her that her Son was not in His tomb, but had risen from the dead. [4] There are many other instances in the Bible of people coming face to face with God's messengers.

But, angels are not just messengers, they have lots of duties... worshipping God, ministering to people, protecting us.

When mankind was made, we were made a little lower than the angels. [5] But, when Christ died for us, we became heirs with Him. [6] That means whatever belongs to Jesus, will also belong to His brothers and sisters... His followers. His angels are sent to minister to us and protect us for God. [7]

But, you never worship angels or put your faith in them. [8] Jesus is the King. The angels belong to Him, just like we belong to Him. Put your faith and trust in God. He is the One who sends the angels.

Have you ever seen an angel? Maybe you have and didn't realize it was an angel. They have appeared to many people. They often have a message from God. But, you must be careful. The devil has transformed himself into an angel of light to fool people more than a few times. [9] If an angel ever visits you, and they bring a message to you, all you have to do is check it out with the Bible. If it goes against what the Bible says, it is not from God. [10]

We all have guardian angels. Some people have even seen theirs. Did you know that in heaven your guardian angel can always see the face of God? [11] That is how important your protection is to Him.

Scriptural References

1   Now in the sixth month the angel Gabriel was sent by God to a city of Galilee named Nazareth, to a virgin betrothed to a man whose name was Joseph, of the house of David. The virgin's name was Mary. Then the angel said to her, "Do not be afraid, Mary, for you have found favor with God. And behold, you will conceive in your womb and bring forth a Son, and shall call His name Jesus. Luke 1:26,27,30,31

2   Then an angel of the Lord appeared to him, standing on the right side of the altar of incense. And when Zacharias saw him, he was troubled, and fear fell upon him. But the angel said to him, "Do not be afraid, Zacharias, for your prayer is heard; and your wife Elizabeth will bear you a son, and you shall call his name John. Luke 1:11-13

3   And He was there in the wilderness forty days, tempted by Satan, and was with the wild beasts; and the angels ministered to Him. Mark 1:13

4   But the angel answered and said to the women, "Do not be afraid, for I know that you seek Jesus who was crucified. "He is not here; for He is risen, as He said. Come, see the place where the Lord lay. Matthew 28:5,6

5   What is man that You are mindful of him, And the son of man that You visit him? For You have made him a little lower than the angels, And You have crowned him with glory and honor. Psalm 8:4,5

6   The Spirit Himself bears witness with our spirit that we are children of God, and if children, then heirs—heirs of God and joint heirs with Christ, if indeed we suffer with Him, that we may also be glorified together. Romans 8:16,17

7   For He shall give His angels charge over you, To keep you in all your ways. Psalm 91:11

8   Let no one cheat you of your reward, taking delight in false humility and worship of angels, intruding into those things which he has not seen, vainly puffed up by his fleshly mind, Collossians 2:18

9   And no wonder! For Satan himself transforms himself into an angel of light. 2 Corinthians 11:14

10 Beloved, do not believe every spirit, but test the spirits, whether they are of God; because many false prophets have gone out into the world. By this you know the Spirit of God: Every spirit that confesses that Jesus Christ has come in the flesh is of God, and every spirit that does not confess that Jesus Christ has come in the flesh is not of God. And this is the spirit of the Antichrist, which you have heard was coming, and is now already in the world. 1 John 4:1-3

11 "Take heed that you do not despise one of these little ones, for I say to you that in heaven their angels always see the face of My Father who is in heaven. Matthew 18:10

Discussion Questions

1) Do we become angels when we die?

(The Bible separates angels and men as different creatures made by the same God. However, our spirits go to heaven and we become like angels.

"For in the resurrection they neither marry nor are given in marriage, but are like angels of God in heaven. (Matthew 22:30)

"nor can they die anymore, for they are equal to the angels and are sons of God, being sons of the resurrection." (Luke 20:36)

"What is man that you are mindful of him, and the son of man that You visit him? For You have made him a little lower than the angels, and You have crowned him with glory and honor." (Psalm 8:4,5)

4) What are some reasons angels appear to people?

(They come to bring good news like the birth of a baby and they bring warnings. For example: the births of Jesus, John the Baptist, & Samson An angel warned Mary and Joseph to leave because Herod was looking to kill Jesus). They appear to people while they are in bad situations (Daniel, in the lions' den, three became four in the fiery furnace). They even come to people as proof of God's existence (Paul, on the way to Damascus, Acts 27:23)

Activity

Directions: Draw and color your own guardian angel.

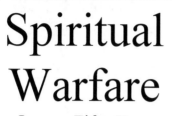

Spiritual Warfare

Lesson Fifty-Two

Scripture of the Week:
Put on the whole armor of God, that you may be able to stand against the wiles of the devil.

Ephesians 6:11

Lesson: We wrestle not against flesh and blood, but against principalities, powers, the rulers of darkness, against spiritual armies of wickedness in heavenly places.[1]

God has an army of angels and the devil has an army of demons. There is a war going on for your soul. Jesus has already beat the devil, so he is mad. What better way to get back at Jesus than to attack and try to destroy someone He loves... you?

But, you have some very powerful weapons against the devil... the armor of God. Picture a suit of armor. Around your waist you have body armor called the truth. This is the knowledge that Jesus died for you and has already won the battle against the devil. He gave you power over the devil, using His name. Your chest is covered with Righteousness. Righteousness is virtue and doing what is right all the time. Jesus gave that Righteousness to you... so that armor doesn't even have a scratch in it. Your feet are covered with the preparation of the gospel of peace. Your gospel boots are made for walking... all over the devil. Above all, you have the shield of faith. So, when the devil shoots his flaming arrows of warfare against you, they just bounce right off your faith shield. On your head is your helmet of salvation. The devil may try to get to your mind, telling you that you have lost your salvation. But, your helmet is guaranteed not to fall off. It is yours to keep forever. Finally, you have the sword of the Spirit, which is the word of God. All the other parts of your armor are for your protection. The sword is what you use to go after the devil and destroy him.[2]

Think about the attacks of the devil. He throws a "spear" of worry at you. You deflect it with that shield of faith. You know that God has everything worked out for you already.

"But, you are a sinner! Don't you remember stealing five dollars from your big brother's piggy bank," the devil shoots an "arrow" of accusation and guilt at you. But, it bounces off your chest plate. "I repented of that sin and asked my brother and Jesus to forgive me." The shine of your righteousness through Jesus is blinding. You have resisted the devil. Blinded, he turns to walk away.

But, you are not done with him yet. You pull out your sword of the Spirit. You give him a dose of his own medicine. He wants to remind you of your past... remind him of his future. "The devil, who deceived them, was cast into the lake of fire and brimstone... where he will be tormented day and night forever and ever."[3] The devil is limping away now. But, you are still not done. You start praising God with heart and soul. And the devil starts running, falling on his face, then getting up and running again.

He is gone for now. But, he has his spies. He'll try hard to figure out what weapon he can form against you next. Don't worry. No weapon formed against you will work,[4] especially now that you have the armor of God.

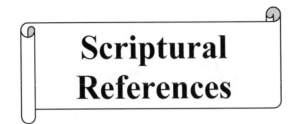

Scriptural References

1   **For we do not wrestle against flesh and blood, but against principalities, against powers, against the rulers of the darkness of this age, against spiritual hosts of wickedness in the heavenly places.   Ephesians 6:12**

2   **Therefore take up the whole armor of God, that you may be able to withstand in the evil day, and having done all, to stand. Stand therefore, having girded your waist with truth, having put on the breastplate of righteousness, and having shod your feet with the preparation of the gospel of peace; above all, taking the shield of faith with which you will be able to quench all the fiery darts of the wicked one. And take the helmet of salvation, and the sword of the Spirit, which is the word of God; Ephesians 6:13-17**

3   **The devil, who deceived them, was cast into the lake of fire and brimstone where the beast and the false prophet are. And they will be tormented day and night forever and ever. Revelation 20:10**

4   **No weapon formed against you shall prosper, And every tongue which rises against you in judgment You shall condemn. This is the heritage of the servants of the LORD, And their righteousness is from Me," Says the LORD.   Isaiah 54:17**

Discussion Questions

1) You have resisted the devil and he fled. So, now do you have to chase him?

(The devil is nothing but a bully. If you have a bully at school and you ignore him, he may leave you alone... at least for the moment. But, he will be back again first chance. But, what happens if you not only resist him, but you beat him until he is black and blue? How willing do you think that devil will be to pick on you if he knows he is going to get his tail whooped?)

2) If you chase the devil, won't that make him mad?

(Who cares?)

3) Can the devil hurt you?

(Only if you let him. The secret is to know that with Christ, you already have the victory over the devil. Jesus won that battle for you. You have much bigger better weapons against him than he has against you, as long as you are a believer. Jesus' name alone is more powerful than anything the devil has in his arsenal.)

Activity

Directions: Draw a picture of yourself wearing the armor of God. Label each piece. (Waist girded with truth, breastplate of righteousness, boots of the gospel of peace, shield of faith, helmet of salvation, and sword of the Spirit)

Reproducible Activity Sheets

Is God Real?

Lesson One Activity

Pretend that your best friend doesn't believe in God. Write a letter to your friend to convince him/her that God exists. Give personal stories of the impact the Lord has made on your life as "proof" that He exists.

_____

_____

_____

_____

_____

_____

_____

_____

_____

_____

_____

_____

_____

_____

_____

SCRIPTURE OF THE WEEK: For since the creation of the world His invisible attributes are clearly seen, being understood by the things that are made, even His eternal power and Godhead, so that they are without excuse, Romans 1:20

God The Father,
Son, and Holy Spirit
Lesson Two Activity

Look at the list below. Figure out Who did what. Then, list it under the proper Name. (Hint: Some things may go under all three!)

GOD, THE FATHER	GOD, THE SON	GOD, THE HOLY SPIRIT
_____	_____	_____
_____	_____	_____
_____	_____	_____
_____	_____	_____
_____	_____	_____
_____	_____	_____
_____	_____	_____
_____	_____	_____

Created heaven and earth
Lives in people's hearts,
    to guide them
Lives in people and
    performs miracles
    through them
You <u>must</u> have a relationship
    with to go to heaven
Died for mankind's sins

Has existed forever
Loves mankind
Lived in Jesus
Will return on the clouds
Causes people to speak in tongues
Is King of kings
Gave the world commandments
Created man

SCRIPTURE OF THE WEEK: "But if I do, though you believe not me, believe the works: that you may know, and believe, that the Father is in me, and I in him." John 10:38

Names of God
Lesson Three Activity

Pick out one of the names of God. Draw and color a picture that reflects that name. (It can be a picture of God or of something showing that part of His personality.) Below is a list of some of God's names.

Creator	Abba Father	Rock	Holy	El-Elyon (Most High God)
Jehovah	Father of lights	Living God	I Am	God of hosts (heavenly army)
Eternal God	Almighty God	Everlasting God		El-Shaddai (God of blessings)

SCRIPTURE OF THE WEEK: And I appeared unto Abraham, unto Isaac, and unto Jacob, by the name of God Almighty, but by my name JEHOVAH was I not known to them. Exodus 6:3

Why God Created Man
Lesson Four Activity

Each symbol represents a letter. "Decode" the message below.

✌=A   👌=B   👍=C   👈=D   👉=E   ✋=F   ☺=G

🔔=H   📖=I   🚩=J   ✈=K   ☼=L   ✉=M   💧=N

❄=O   ✝=P   ☥=Q   ✠=R   ✡=S   ⏳=T   🖱=U

❁=V   🕯=W   ✏=X   ✍=Y   ✂=Z

___G O D___   ___I S___   ___F A I T H F U L___   ___B Y___

___W H O M___   ___Y O U___   ___W E R E___

___C A L L E D___   ___I N T O___   ___T H E___

___F E L L O W S H I P___   ___O F___   ___H I S___

___S O N___   ___J E S U S___   ___C H R I S T___

___O U R___   ___L O R D___   1 Corinthians 1:9

Creation of the Earth
Lesson Five Activity

God created all the animals and Adam named them. Now it is your turn. In the space below create your own animal and color it. When you are finished, name it.

SCRIPTURE OF THE WEEK: The earth is the Lord's, and all its fullness, The world and those who dwell therein. Psalm 24:1

222

The Fall of Man
Lesson Six Activity

Directions: Adam and Eve both blamed someone else for their own mistake. Think about a time that you have blamed someone else for something that you did wrong (even if they was also their fault.) Write about that time.

_____

_____

_____

_____

_____

_____

_____

_____

_____

How could you have handled it differently?

_____

_____

_____

_____

_____

SCRIPTURE OF THE WEEK: Blessed are those who do His commandments, that they may have the right to the tree of life, and may enter through the gates into the city. Revelation 22:14

Noah and His Ark

Lesson Seven Activity

E	I	W	H	A	L	E	S	E	T	E	V	O	D	M	Y
L	R	A	I	N	B	O	W	G	N	O	I	L	I	N	E
T	T	H	E	C	L	O	U	D	I	A	R	B	E	Z	S
R	A	N	D	E	R	E	G	I	T	P	X	A	P	E	R
U	M	R	O	W	A	K	O	A	L	A	O	B	I	T	O
T	S	H	A	L	L	G	K	W	A	H	F	M	B	E	H
F	O	R	T	H	E	T	L	G	O	A	T	A	G	O	D
J	A	G	U	A	R	A	✠	E	W	O	C	L	T	A	C
S	I	G	N	O	F	B	T	H	E	Y	E	K	N	O	M
L	C	O	V	E	N	A	N	T	G	D	O	N	K	E	Y
A	B	E	T	W	E	E	N	M	E	O	M	O	U	S	E
E	G	O	O	S	E	N	E	V	A	R	R	L	L	U	B
S	A	N	D	T	H	E	E	A	R	T	H	F	M	A	R

Find the animal words hidden in the puzzle. When you find an animal word, mark through it (instead of circling it). Once you have found all of the words, try to figure out the message that remains. Use the space below to write the message.

_____

_____

FIND THESE WORDS

WHALE	TIGER	JAGUAR	APE
DOVE	FOX	MONKEY	COW
TURTLE	WORM	SEAL	LAMB
PIG	GOOSE	MOUSE	RAM
DONKEY	CAT	DOG	FROG
LION	BAT	GOAT	KOALA
HORSE	BULL	EAGLE	
ZEBRA	RAVEN	HAWK	

224

Moses and the Big Ten
Lesson Eight Activity

"Decode" the pictures and fill in the blanks.

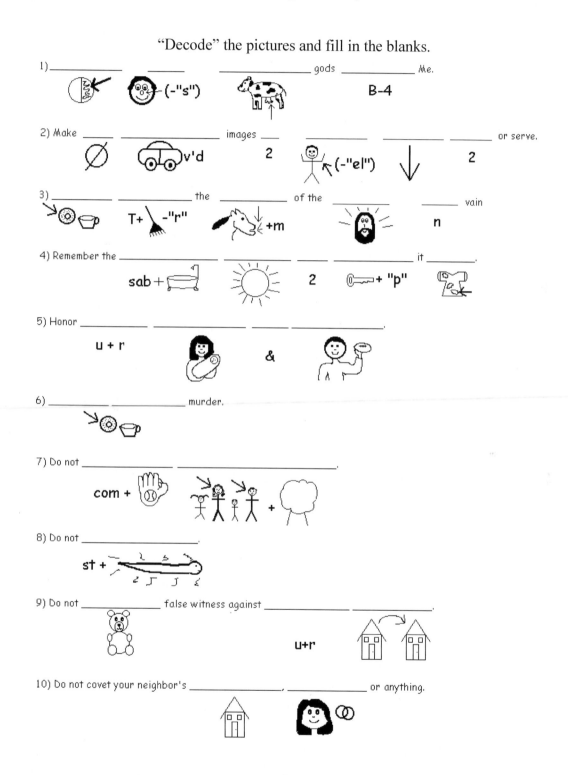

1) _____ _____ _____ gods _____ Me.

2) Make ____ ____ images ____ ____ ____ or serve.

3) _____ _____ the _____ of the _____ _____ vain

4) Remember the _____ _____ _____ _____ it _____.

5) Honor _____ _____ _____.

6) _____ _____ murder.

7) Do not _____ _____.

8) Do not _____.

9) Do not _____ false witness against _____ _____.

10) Do not covet your neighbor's _____, _____ or anything.

SCRIPTURE OF THE WEEK: Blessed are those who do His commandments, that they may have the right to the tree of life, and may enter through the gates into the city. Revelation 22:14

Tithing
Lesson Nine Activity

List as many things as you can think of to tithe to God.

_____   _____

_____   _____

_____   _____

_____   _____

_____   _____

What are some special things that *you* have to tithe to the kingdom of God?

_____   _____

_____   _____

_____   _____

SCRIPTURE OF THE WEEK: Bring all the tithes into the storehouse, That there may be food in My house,... Malachi 3:10

Worshipping God... Why?

Lesson Ten

There are many things that God does for us. How many reasons can you think of to praise God? What are some things that you are thankful for?

_____

_____

_____

_____

_____

_____

_____

_____

_____

_____

_____

_____

_____

_____

SCRIPTURE OF THE WEEK: Let everything that has breath praise the Lord. Praise the Lord! Psalm 150:6

Worshipping God with Our Mouths

Lesson Eleven Activity

Complete the crossword puzzle.

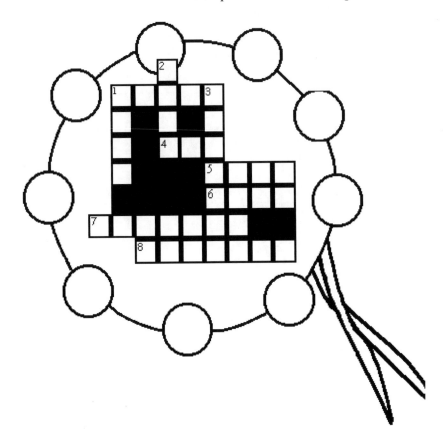

DOWN

1) What do you do with your voice, set to music?
2) The Lord is _____.
3) Sound the _____! (a musical instrument)

ACROSS

1) God has gone up with a…
4) Whom did Jesus die for?
5) You _____ believe in Jesus to be saved.
6) When you talk to God, you____ ____
7) If you are baptized with the Spirit, you can pray in _____.
8) When you praise God, you _____ the devil.

SCRIPTURE OF THE WEEK: God has gone up with a shout, The LORD with the sound of a trumpet. Sing praises to God, sing praises! Sing praises to our King, sing praises! Psalms 47: 5,6

Worshipping God with Our Hands and Feet
Lesson Twelve Activity

Make up a song (or cheer) and a dance (or cheer movements) to praise God. You can make it short and sweet, if you would like. Now, perform it for the class. Put some spirit into it!

_____

_____

_____

_____

_____

_____

_____

_____

_____

_____

_____

_____

_____

_____

_____

SCRIPTURE OF THE WEEK: I desire therefore that the men pray everywhere, lifting up holy hands, without wrath of doubting. 1 Timothy 2:8

Worshipping God with Our Lives
Lesson Thirteen Activity

List all of your favorite things to do.

_____   _____

_____   _____

_____   _____

_____   _____

Now, look at these activities individually. How can you use each of these bring glory to God?

Pick out a two or three of your very favorite of these. Write down how you can use these to further the Kingdom of God.

_____

_____

_____

_____

_____

_____

_____

_____

_____

_____

_____

SCRIPTURE OF THE WEEK: "But the hour is coming, and now is, when the true worshipers will worship the Father in spirit and truth; for the Father is seeking such to worship Him. John 4:23

The Power of the Name of Jesus
Lesson Fourteen Activity

Unscramble the words that describe some of the things that the power of the Name of Jesus can do. When you have unscrambled all of the words. Insert the words in parentheses ( ) in the puzzle below. You will find the Name that is above all names.

1) (dugej) webneet tigrh dan grown _____

2) (leah) _____

3) (ydserot) taans _____

4) vome (tinsomuna) _____

5) ganech (slevi) _____

1)   ☐ _ _ _ _ _

2)   _ ☐ _ _ _

3)   _ _ ☐ _ _ _ _ _

4)   _ _ ☐ _ _ _ _ _ _

5)   _ _ _ _ ☐

SCRIPTURE OF THE WEEK: "And whatever you ask in My name, that I will do, that the Father may be glorified in the Son. John 14:13

231

Using God's Word
Lesson Fifteen Activity

The Bible is full of God's promises. Name as many of God's promises as you can.

_____

_____

_____

_____

_____

_____

Draw (and color) a picture of God fulfilling one of His promises.

SCRIPTURE OF THE WEEK: For let him ask in faith, with no doubting, for he who doubts is like a wave of the sea driven and tossed by the wind. James 1: 6

When to Pray
Lesson Sixteen Activity

Write a letter to God. You can thank Him, let Him know what you are feeling and thinking, whatever you want to talk to Him about. This is just between you and Him.

Dear God,

_____

_____

_____

_____

_____

_____

_____

_____

_____

_____

_____

_____

_____

_____

Love Your child,

_____

SCRIPTURE OF THE WEEK: Pray without ceasing. 1 Thessalonians 5:17

Why Jesus Came
Lesson Seventeen

Directions: "Decode" the message.

= A   = B   = C   = D   = E   = F   = G

= H   = I   = J   = K   = L   = M   = N

= O   = P   = Q   = R   = S   = T   = U   = V

= W   = X   = Y   = Z

_____

_____

_____

_____

_____

John 18:37

The Birth of Christ
Lesson Eighteen Activity

Pretend that you are a reporter and you have just visited the Christ Child in the stable. Write a story for your newspaper explaining what you saw and what it means to the world. Don't forget the catchy headline!

_____

_____

_____

_____

_____

_____

_____

_____

_____

_____

_____

_____

_____

SCRIPTURE OF THE WEEK: **"For there is born to you this day in the city of David a Savior, who is Christ the Lord. Luke 2:11**

The Baptism of Jesus
Lesson Nineteen Activity

Immediately after Jesus was baptized, the Holy Spirit descended on Him like a dove. Draw and color this scene as you imagine it looked.

SCRIPTURE OF THE WEEK: ...“Repent for the kingdom of heaven is at hand.” Matthew 3:2

Temptation by Satan
Lesson Twenty Activity

Fill in the blanks. You will find what you should do when the devil tempts you.

1) How many days did Jesus fast?
2) Satan tried to get Jesus to turn the stones into _____.
3) Who led Jesus into the wilderness?
4) What caused the devil to have control of the kingdoms of the world?
5) _____ came to minister to Jesus after the devil left.
6) Jesus answered the devil by quoting _____.

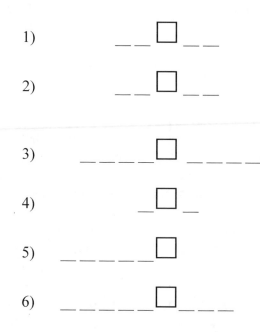

1)   _ _ ☐ _ _

2)   _ _ ☐ _ _

3)   _ _ _ _ ☐ _ _ _ _ _

4)   _ ☐ _

5)   _ _ _ _ _ ☐

6)   _ _ _ _ _ ☐ _ _ _

... the devil and he will flee from you. James 4:7

Jesus Comes to Town
Lesson Twenty-One Activity

Act out the story of Jesus coming to town.

It was a cool, sunny morning. Passover was just a few days away. Jesus and his disciples were just outside the village of Bethany. The disciples thought they were going into Jerusalem to celebrate the Passover feast. But, Jesus knew the real reason He was there. He was going there to die.

After breakfast, Jesus sent two of His disciples into a nearby village. He told them, "As soon as you enter the village, you will see the colt of a donkey tied up. Bring it to me. If anyone asks you, tell them it is for Your Lord and they will let you have it."

So, the men went into the village and found the colt, just as Jesus said. But, the people saw them untying the colt and asked them what they were doing. The disciples told them, "The Lord has need of it." So, they let him have it. Word quickly spread throughout the villages that Jesus was coming to town.

The disciples brought the donkey to Jesus. They put their clothes on the donkey's back, and helped Jesus on it. The slow ride into Jerusalem began. By the time Jesus came down the hill, the townspeople had made a path for him. They had spread out their clothes and palm branches all over the path, to honor him. That is why the Sunday before Easter is called "Palm Sunday," to celebrate Jesus' triumphant entrance into Jerusalem.

The people were so excited to see Jesus, they cried out, "Hosanna to the Son of David! Blessed is He who comes in the name of the Lord! Hosanna in the highest!"

The chief priests and the scribes were angry and jealous. They didn't like the idea of Jesus getting all the attention. They told Him to tell the crowd to be quiet.

But Jesus replied, "If they were quiet, the very stones would cry out in praise." Jesus knew that He was the Son of God. And he knew that by honoring Him, the people were also honoring God.

Jesus looked on the beautiful city, then wept. He was very sad. He knew that soon the whole city would be destroyed and all the people within it, because Jerusalem did not recognize the day that God came to save it. (Some thirty-seven years later, in AD 70, the Romans did destroy Jerusalem.)

Jesus and his disciples spent the night at their friends, Mary, Martha, and Lazarus', house in Bethany. The following morning, a Monday, Jesus went back into Jerusalem. This time, he went into the temple. It was once again filled with moneychangers and traders.

Jesus had cleared out the temple once before. Today He was filled with righteous anger. He turned over their tables, as he spoke God's word, "It is written, that God's House shall be a house of prayer for all nations; but your have made it into a den of thieves."

Once Jesus had cleared the temple, He began teaching and healing in it once again. The people hung on His every word. This made the chief priests and the scribes very mad. So, they tried to figure out a way to destroy Jesus and His works, once and for all.

SCRIPTURE OF THE WEEK: Tell the daughter of Zion, 'Behold your King is coming to you, Lowly, and sitting on a donkey, A colt, the foal of a donkey.'" Matthew 21:5

The Last Days of Jesus
Lesson Twenty-Two Activity

Draw and color a picture of something that happened during the last days of Jesus (last supper, praying in the garden, the crowd coming to get Jesus, Jesus healing the man's ear, etc.)

SCRIPTURE OF THE WEEK: "Watch and pray, lest you enter into temptation. The spirit indeed is willing, but the flesh is weak." Matthew 26:41

The Resurrection
Lesson Twenty-Three Activity

Draw and color a picture of something in this lesson (Jesus being tried, Jesus carrying the cross, Jesus on the cross, Jesus rising from the grave, Mary and Mary finding the empty tomb, etc.)

SCRIPTURE OF THE WEEK: "But when you give a feast, invite the poor, the maimed, the lame, the blind. "And you will be blessed, because they cannot repay you; for you shall be repaid at the resurrection of the just." Luke 14: 13,14

Jesus Sends the Holy Spirit
Lesson Twenty-Four Activity

Think back over your life. Have you ever had a very strong feeling that you believe may have been from the Holy Spirit. Describe the event (or events) where you believe you heard from God... where He used the Holy Spirit to teach, warn, guide, or communicate with you.

_____

_____

_____

_____

_____

_____

_____

_____

_____

_____

_____

_____

_____

_____

SCRIPTURE OF THE WEEK: And I will pray the Father, and He will give you another Helper, that He may abide with your forever. John 14:16

Jesus Rules and Reigns

Lesson Twenty-Five Activity

Draw and color a picture of Jesus on His throne, ruling the universe.

SCRIPTURE OF THE WEEK: For by Him all things were created that are in heaven and that are on earth, visible and invisible, whether thrones or dominions or principalities or powers. All things were created through Him and for Him. Colossians 1:16

When Jesus Returns
Lesson Twenty-Six

Write a short story about the day Jesus returns. You can include how it looks, stories of the people left behind and what they are thinking, etc.

_____

_____

_____

_____

_____

_____

_____

_____

_____

_____

_____

_____

_____

_____

_____

_____

SCRIPTURE OF THE WEEK: "Watch therefore, for you know neither the day nor the hour in which the Son of Man is coming." Matthew 25:13

Love
Lesson Twenty-Seven

Make up and act out a skit showing the fruit of the Spirit, Love. This page may be used to write down your lines, acting notes, etc.

_____

_____

_____

_____

_____

_____

_____

_____

_____

_____

_____

_____

_____

_____

SCRIPTURE OF THE WEEK: "But I say to you, love your enemies, bless those who curse you, do good to those who hate you, and pray for those who spitefully use you and persecute you" Matt 5:44

Joy
Lesson Twenty-Eight

How many ways can you name to spread the Joy of the Lord?

_____

_____

_____

_____

_____

_____

_____

_____

_____

_____

_____

_____

_____

_____

SCRIPTURE OF THE WEEK: ...this day is holy unto our Lord: neither be ye sorry; for the joy of the LORD is your strength. Nehemiah 8:10

Peace
Lesson Twenty-Nine Activity

Write down everything that you ever worry about. When you are finished give your worries to God. Put the list in the collection plate or leave it at the altar railing.

_____

_____

_____

_____

_____

_____

_____

_____

_____

_____

_____

_____

_____

_____

_____

SCRIPTURE OF THE WEEK: Let the peace of God rule in your hearts... Colossians 3:15

Longsuffering
Lesson Thirty Activity

B	F	Y	Q	Y	O	G	U	F	R
F	P	W	A	T	G	I	F	E	N
G	C	E	P	O	D	S	S	D	F
E	S	G	W	G	F	Q	F	W	D
Q	G	F	Y	O	Q	U	F	G	R
W	S	Q	O	U	F	L	S	W	Q

Follow the directions below. You will be left with a message from Luke 21:19. Write the message here.

_____

_____

1) If Jesus saves, cross out all of the Q's.
If you don't need Jesus to get to heaven, cross out all the S's.

2) If God is impatient with us, cross out all the E's.
If God is patient with us, cross out all the D's.

3) If it is OK to use God's name in vain, cross out all the P's.
If it is a sin to use God's name in vain, cross out all the W's.

5) If it is OK not to forgive someone who has sinned against you for the seventh time, cross out all the Y's.
If God expects us to forgive someone seventy times seven times, cross out all the F's.

5) If patience (longsuffering) is a fruit of the Spirit, cross out all the G's.
If patience (longsuffering) is a fruit of sin, cross out all the A's.

Gentleness and Kindness

Lesson Thirty-One Activity

Jesus told a story about the gentleness and kindness shown by a good Samaritan. Act out the story. Use the bottom of this page to write down your lines if you need to.

The Good Samaritan

"A certain *man* went down from Jerusalem to Jericho, and fell among thieves, who stripped him of his clothing, wounded *him,* and departed, leaving *him* half dead. "Now by chance a certain priest came down that road. And when he saw him, he passed by on the other side. "Likewise a Levite, when he arrived at the place, came and looked, and passed by on the other side. "But a certain Samaritan, as he journeyed, came where he was. And when he saw him, he had compassion. "So he went to *him* and bandaged his wounds, pouring on oil and wine; and he set him on his own animal, brought him to an inn, and took care of him. "On the next day, when he departed, he took out two denarii, gave *them* to the innkeeper, and said to him, 'Take care of him; and whatever more you spend, when I come again, I will repay you.'"

Luke 10:30-36

_____

_____

_____

_____

_____

_____

_____

_____

SCRIPTURE OF THE WEEK: "So which of these three do you think was neighbor to him who fell among the thieves?" And he said, "He who showed mercy on him." Then Jesus said to him, "Go and do likewise."

Goodness
Lesson Thirty-Two Activity

Describe a "good" person. You might tell what a "good" person does, how you can tell if someone is good, etc.

_____

_____

_____

_____

_____

_____

_____

_____

_____

_____

_____

_____

_____

_____

_____

SCRIPTURE OF THE WEEK: Every good gift and every perfect gift is from above, and comes down from the Father of lights, with whom there is no variation of shadow of turning. James 1:17

Faithfulness
Lesson Thirty-Three Activity

Draw a picture of when Peter loses His faith in Jesus. Then draw a picture of what would have happened if Peter had not lost his faith.

SCRIPTURE OF THE WEEK: ...the just shall live by his faith. Habakkuk 2:4

250

Self Control
Lesson Thirty-Four Activity

List as many things as you can think of that make you lose self-control... things that tempt you.

_____

_____

_____

_____

_____

_____

Now write down the ways you <u>should</u> deal with these things and how you <u>actually</u> deal with them.

_____

_____

_____

_____

_____

_____

_____

_____

_____

SCRIPTURE OF THE WEEK: For where your treasure is, there your heart will be also. Luke 12:34

What are the Gifts?
Lesson Thirty-Five Activity

Unscramble the words to find the gifts of the Holy Spirit.

stoptreetrainin = _____

gotuens = _____

mcarlies = _____

glahein = _____

gednicrisn fo tirssip = _____

doswim = _____

gleendkow = _____

tihaf = _____

chopprey = _____

SCRIPTURE OF THE WEEK: But the manifestation of the Spirit is give to each one for the profit of all. 1 Corinthians 12:7

Evidence of the Baptism
of the Holy Spirit
Lesson Thirty-Six Activity

Take this time to lay hands on each other and (for those who wish) pray for the baptism of the Holy Spirit. If no one wishes for the baptism of the Holy Spirit, pray for each other anyway. Remember that all you need to do to receive the baptism of the Holy Spirit is to want it, pray for it, and believe that you have received it. No one will force you to speak in tongues. If you want to once you have received the baptism of the Holy Spirit, you have to make the noise, but the Holy Spirit will give you the words. If you have any special prayer requests, write them down here. When it is your turn to be prayed for, you can read this aloud, if you want, to the people praying for you. Or you can just tell your classmates, "I need prayer," without telling them what about. You might want to write down other's prayer requests here, too. That way you can take this home and pray for them later too.

_____

_____

_____

_____

_____

_____

_____

_____

_____

_____

_____

SCRIPTURE OF THE WEEK: **"And these signs will follow those who believe: In My name they will cast out demons; they will speak with new tongues; Mark 16:17**

Tongues / Interpretations
Lesson Thirty-Seven Activity

A	T	H	E	R	E	F	O	R	E	S	M
N	G	O	D	T	O	N	G	U	E	G	I
G	S	J	A	R	E	Y	L	O	H	N	R
E	H	E	F	O	R	A	W	S	I	I	A
L	E	S	G	N	N	O	I	T	T	L	C
S	A	U	O	T	H	O	S	S	E	A	L
W	V	S	H	O	B	E	D	L	I	E	E
E	E	V	E	B	U	T	O	T	O	H	S
U	N	N	B	E	L	I	M	E	V	E	R

Find the words hidden in the puzzle. When you find a word, mark through it (instead of circling it). Once you have found all of the words, try to figure out the message that remains. Use the space below to write the message.

_____

_____

_____

1 Corinthians 14:22

FIND THESE WORDS

ANGELS   MIRACLES   HOLY   JESUS   GOD   HEAVEN   WISDOM   HEALINGS

Prophecy
Lesson Thirty-Eight Activity

Tell a story about someone who pretended they had the gift of prophecy, but really didn't. What harm could someone like that cause, who might believe in them, how were they "found out" as a fake?

_____

_____

_____

_____

_____

_____

_____

_____

_____

_____

_____

_____

_____

_____

_____

_____

SCRIPTURE OF THE WEEK: For false christs and false prophets will rise and show signs and wonders to deceive, if possible, even the elect. Mark 13:22

Faith
Lesson Thirty-Nine Activity

What is your biggest dream? Your heart's desire? Is it to be a doctor? To get a little sister? To fly to the moon? Whatever it is, it will take faith to let God show you the way to your heart's desire. Write down whatever it is you want more than anything else in the world. Explain why you want it and how you believe getting it will affect your life. Be sure to put today's date on it!

_____
(date)

_____

_____

_____

_____

_____

_____

_____

_____

_____

_____

_____

Take this home and keep it. Talk to God about it. See if you can find a scripture or two that relates to it and write them down here too. Have faith that God's will is going to be done in your life. Pull this out from time to time and pray about it again. When you feel you have received God's answer about it, write down the answer on this page too. Answered prayers help build your faith.

SCRIPTURE OF THE WEEK: So the Lord said, "If you have faith as a mustard seed, you can say to this mulberry tree, 'Be pulled up by the roots and be planted in the sea,' and it would obey you. Luke 17:6

Healing
Lesson Forty Activity

Do you have any illnesses or disabilities that you want God to heal? Or maybe you have a relative or a friend who needs healing? Write down whatever it is on this paper. Don't worry, you don't have to show anyone. You can fold it and stick it in your pocket if you want. God can still see it. Now, pray with your classmates about it. And pray about the things your friends need too. Most of all have faith that God loves you enough to answer your prayer.

_____

_____

_____

_____

_____

_____

_____

_____

Here are a few promises of God on the subject of healing. If you prayed with your class about someone you love that needs healing, you should share these scriptures with them too.

But to you who fear My Name The Sun of Righteousness shall arise with healing in His wings... Malachi 4:2

O Lord My God, I cried to You and You have healed me. O Lord, You brought my soul up from the grave; You have kept me alive, that I should not go down to the pit. Psalm 30:2,3

The Lord will strengthen him on his bed of illness; You will sustain him on his sickbed. Psalm 41:3

He sent His word and healed them, And delivered them from their destructions. Psalm 107:20

SCRIPTURE OF THE WEEK: But He was wounded for our transgressions, He was bruised for our iniquities; the chastisement for our peace was upon Him, and by His stripes we are healed. Isaiah 53:5

Miracles
Lesson Forty-One Activity

Write a story about someone who <u>really</u> needed a miracle, prayed for it, believed for it, and received it.

_____

_____

_____

_____

_____

_____

_____

_____

_____

_____

_____

Do you, or someone you know, <u>really need</u> a miracle. Write down what you think you (or they) need here. Pray about it. See if you can find a promise of God relating to it and write that down here too. Keep on praying and believing until you feel you have received an answer from God. Remember sometimes the miracle we <u>think</u> we need, turns out to be different than the miracle we <u>really need.</u>

_____

_____

_____

SCRIPTURE OF THE WEEK: But Jesus said, "Do not forbid him, for no one who works a miracle in My name can soon afterward speak evil of Me. Mark 9:39

Knowledge

Lesson Forty-Two Activity

Directions: "Decode" the message.

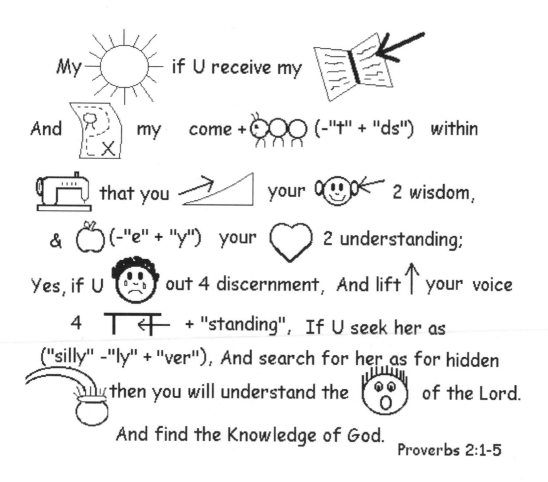

My ☀ if U receive my 📖

And 📝 my come + 🐜🐜🐜 (-"t" + "ds") within

🧵 that you ↗ your 👁 2 wisdom,

& 🍎(-"e" + "y") your ♡ 2 understanding;

Yes, if U 🙁 out 4 discernment, And lift ↑ your voice

4 ⊤⇐ + "standing", If U seek her as

("silly" -"ly" + "ver"), And search for her as for hidden

🏺 then you will understand the 😮 of the Lord.

And find the Knowledge of God.

Proverbs 2:1-5

_____

_____

_____

_____

259

Wisdom
Lesson Forty-Three Activity

Name as many things as you can think of that someone your age can do to help the Kingdom of God grow?

_____

_____

_____

_____

_____

_____

_____

_____

_____

_____

_____

_____

_____

_____

_____

SCRIPTURE OF THE WEEK: Wisdom is the principal thing; therefore get wisdom. And in all your getting, get understanding. Proverbs 4:7

Discerning of Spirits
Lesson Forty-Four Activity

Can you match up which spirits are operating in each story?

1) Susie and Rachel are best friends. But a new girl, Angie just moved in next door to Susie. Susie and Rachel are making plans to go to the movies this Saturday. Susie suggests they invite Angie along. Rachel lies and tells Susie that she really doesn't think there will be room for Angie in her mom's car, so they can't invite her.

_____

2) Timothy just moved into a new house. He is trying to go to sleep, but he keeps hearing strange noises. He gets up and checks the closet, under the bed, and behind the door... again. He hasn't been afraid of the dark since he was little. But, he just can't help feeling this way.

_____

3) Things weren't the same at the church youth group anymore. Everyone used to get along great, but lately everyone has been fighting over stupid little things.

_____

4) Ramona started going to a new school. She saw a group of girls in her math class that she thought she might say hello to. But, just as she was about to try to make friends with them, they all started laughing. Ramona was sure they were laughing at her. So she didn't try to make friends with them after all. What she didn't know was that they were laughing about a TV show they had watched the night before.

_____

5) Cameron was in church. They were playing one of his favorite praise songs. But, this time he couldn't praise God. He just kept thinking that he must look stupid clapping his hands in church.

_____

Choose from these evil spirits...

spirit of division   spirit of jealousy

spirit of fear   spirit of fear of rejection

spirits of the antichrist & pride

SCRIPTURE OF THE WEEK: Then they were all amazed, so that they questioned among themselves, saying, "What is this? What new doctrine is this? For with authority He commands even the unclean sprits, and they obey Him. Mark 1:27

Silly Looking Things
Lesson Forty-Five Activity

Name all the "silly" looking things you have seen people do and why they do them. Which of these things don't seem silly unless you see people do them in church?

_____

_____

_____

_____

_____

_____

_____

_____

_____

_____

Why do you think things that usually look fine where people do them (like jumping up and down at a football game) seem very strange if they are done in church?

_____

_____

_____

_____

SCRIPTURE OF THE WEEK: But God hath chosen the foolish things of the world to confound the wise; and God hath chosen the weak things of the world to confound the things which are mighty. 1 Corinthians 1:27

Witnessing to the World
By Your Actions
Lesson Forty-Six Activity

Are you being a good ambassador for Christ? Take a little quiz to see how you are doing. Be honest with your answers. Don't just choose what you think is the "right" answer. Choose what you <u>really do</u>. No one will see this quiz, unless you show it to them.

1) You are with your friends trying on clothes. You find a great T-shirt that you decide to buy with your birthday money, but when you are taking it off you get something on it. It will probably come off in the wash. What do you do?

    A) Buy it anyway. You are positive it will wash out.

    B) Put it back and get a different one. You know the store can't sell it like that, but they have all kinds of money. Losing money on one T-shirt won't hurt them.

    C) Show the T-shirt to the sales clerk and ask for a discount because it's dirty, never mentioning that you are the one who got it dirty.

    D) Show the T-shirt to the sales clerk, tell her you were the one who got it dirty, and see what she says. You really don't want to buy a shirt with something on it, but you are willing to pay for the damage that you caused to it.

2) Your best friend invites you to go to water park with her on Saturday. But, you have already promised your little brother that you would teach him to ride his bike without training wheels Saturday. What do you do?

    A) Ask your friend if you can go with her a different day, you already have plans to teach your little brother how to ride his bike

    B) Ask your friend if your little brother can go along too. You can teach him next weekend if you all go to the water park this weekend.

    C) Tell your little brother that you don't have time to help him. It's your parent's responsibility anyway.

    D) Completely blow off your little brother. He was a jerk to you the other day anyway. You don't owe him an explanation. Just leave with your friend.

3) You are walking through the mall doors. About fifteen feet away you see a woman pushing a stroller and dragging along a two-year-old by the hand. You could hold open the door for her, but it looks like it is going to take her another minute to get to it and your friends are already half way to the fountain. What do you do?

    A) You let the door go and catch up with your friends. You don't want them to leave you behind. Besides, the woman had the kids, they are her responsibility.

    B) You pretend you don't see her and run to catch up with your friends.

    C) You stand there and keep holding the door open for her.

    D) You hold the door open for a minute. But, it starts taking her too long to get there, so you let it go. She should have hurried.

SCRIPTURE OF THE WEEK: Let no one despise your youth, but be an example to the believers in word, in conduct, in love, in spirit, in faith, in purity. 1 Timothy 4:12

263

Witnessing to the World
Friends and Family
Lesson Forty-Seven Activity

Pretend that you are the only Christian in your group of friends or in your family. You want your loved ones to join you in heaven one day. In the hopes that they too will turn their lives over to Christ, you realize you must really "let your Jesus show." Write and act out a skit of someone witnessing to their friends or family by "letting their Jesus show."

_____

_____

_____

_____

_____

_____

_____

_____

_____

_____

_____

_____

SCRIPTURE OF THE WEEK: And let us not grow weary while doing good, for in due season we shall reap if we do not lose heart. Galatians 6:9

Witnessing to the World
Missions
Lesson Forty-Eight Activity

Write a story about a kid your age who goes on a missionary trip (with parents, youth group, etc).

_____

_____

_____

_____

_____

_____

_____

_____

_____

_____

_____

_____

_____

_____

SCRIPTURE OF THE WEEK: Go therefore and make disciples of all the nations, baptizing them in the name of the Father and of the Son and of the Holy Spirit. Matthew 28:19

Is the Devil Real?
Lesson Forty-Nine Activity

Draw a picture of you crushing the devil's head.

SCRIPTURE OF THE WEEK: Above all, taking the shield of faith with which you will be able to quench all the fiery darts of the wicked one. Ephesians 6:16

Christis in the Fire with Us

Lesson Fifty Activity

Draw and color a picture of Shadrach, Meshach, and Abed-Nego, with Jesus, in the fiery furnace.

SCRIPTURE OF THE WEEK: "Be strong and of good courage, do not fear nor be afraid of them; for the Lord your God, He *is* the One who goes with you. He will not leave you nor forsake you." Deuteronomy 31:6

Angels
Lesson Fifty-One Activity

Draw and color your own guardian angel.

SCRIPTURE OF THE WEEK: For He shall give His angels charge over you, To keep you in all your ways. In their hands they shall bear you up, Lest you dash your foot against a stone. Psalm 91:11,12

Spiritual Warfare
Lesson Fifty-Two Activity

Draw a picture of yourself wearing the armor of God. Label each piece. (Waist girded with truth, breastplate of righteousness, boots of gospel of peace, shield of faith, helmet of salvation, and sword of the Spirit)

SCRIPTURE OF THE WEEK: Put on the whole armor of God, that you may be able to stand against the wiles of the devil. Ephesians 6:11

About the Author

As a Children's Ministry Director, Gloria Clawson was frustrated at the lack of curricula available for Spirit-filled churches. After much prayer, she felt let to write ***The Fire of God Series.***

Gloria and her husband have three young sons that remind her daily of the importance of teaching the Word of God.

Printed in the United States
by Baker & Taylor Publisher Services